NO PROPS
no problem

150+ Outrageously Fun Group Games
& Activities using No Equipment

MARK COLLARD

www.playmeo.com

Published by Mark Collard, Director, playmeo Pty Ltd
PO Box 4237, Croydon Hills VIC 3136 Australia
hello@playmeo.com

ABN 53 155 715 656

 A catalogue record for this book is available from the National Library of Australia.

Collard, Mark, 1964-
No Props, No Problem
First edition 2018

ISBN 978-0-9925464-2-7 (paperback)

Illustrations by Anna Rampelt
Book cover & internal layout design by Squeezebox
Photos by Morrison Photography

Printed by IngramSpark

Group games & activities are
fun
playful
attractive
engaging
inviting
insightful
inspiring
adventurous
hilarious
and embody some of the most joyous times of my life.

This book is for those who know this to be true.

And to Gill and Devon,
my love forever and always.

Contents

A book is a book.

When coupled with three extraordinary digital resources, *this* book stands apart.

Happily, these resources are
free
simple
ever-expanding
accessible
exclusive
and will help bring this book alive.

playmeo Group Games app

Available from your favourite app marketplace – **iOS & Android** – 100% free.

The app curates all of playmeo's free content, including dozens of free group games, video tutorials, leadership tips and weekly blog posts. Search **playmeo** and install today.

Online Group Games & Activities Database

Visit playmeo.com and view dozens of fun group games & activities with and without props.

Browse dozens of designated free activities, no opt-in or credit card or required.

Go to **playmeo.com/activities**

QR Code

Hover the QR code reader of your smartphone over the square B&W matrix that accompanies every activity described in this book to open a ton of new content. Video tutorials, leadership tips, reflection strategies and so much more.

Browse for free or subscribe to unlock premium content.

Go to **playmeo.com/signup**

Introduction

"A good idea doesn't care who it belongs to."
– Karl Rohnke, best-selling author of 'Silver Bullets'

Everyone loves a good idea.

Actually, if we're completely honest, what we really want is a *lot* of good ideas – why just stop at one?

And, in the program leadership field, the best ideas are those activities which can be presented quickly, with little effort, are simple to use and generate lots of good outcomes.

Consider the following moments when you wished you had a bunch of good ideas to dip into. Try to catch yourself thinking about the last time one or more of them happened to you:

- You have five minutes to fill before the start of the next session, class, camp, etc.
- Your group has that "We're bored, what are we going to doooo...?" look on their faces.
- The equipment you so meticulously stored last night is now missing, or worse, just broke.
- The clipboard you are holding is worth slightly more than your program's annual budget.
- Your out-of-doors program has just been washed out.
- You simply want to have an outrageously fun time.

This book of ideas is dedicated to these very moments.

There can be no more valuable resource than a large repertoire of activities that can be pulled out of your back-pocket on cue, anytime, anywhere. That's what this book is all about. It is full of dozens of sure-fire, high-energy, interactive, leave-them-asking-for-more games and activities – all of which require no equipment whatsoever.

My original intentions were to simply share a list of the best 'no prop' style activities that I had lead and/or experienced. But, much like the preparation of a yummy meal, no matter how good the ingredients are, the success of the meal will rely heavily on a good recipe.

Accordingly, a series of 'fun' activities played one after the other does not necessarily create a fun and successful experience for everyone. The key is the approach that is taken in the design and delivery of the activities and the program.

So, to help you get the most from this book, here is a sneak preview of what you will discover and learn within this how-to guide, broken into three distinct parts.

Part One: Powerful Program Design

In this part, I share some of the most valuable insights, tools and lessons I have learned that, together, have helped me design and deliver remarkably fun programs that have made a difference to the tens of thousands of people I have worked with all over the world.

First, I share three important truths about program design and leadership which are absolutely essential to making a difference in the life and performance of your groups. These truths form the bedrock of the approach which have fuelled the success I have enjoyed over the years. They are simple, universally applicable and – most importantly – scientifically researched and proven.

I discuss the importance of intentionally building trusting and healthy relationships, and the benefits of taking fun more seriously. As I say, approach is everything – to the extent that two people with similar backgrounds and qualifications may lead the same experience with the same group, yet achieve two completely different outcomes. As you will learn, environment dictates performance.

To this end, I will describe five tools essential to creating the sort of environment that will positively influence the behaviours and performance of your groups. Having fun is key. Honouring choice, valuing people and providing opportunities for growth and interaction with others are also critically important.

These tools, when wrapped in a powerful program framework, will not only prepare your group for what they came for, but help satisfy many of their most basic human needs. I call this framework *The Difference Model* – it's not the truth, it's something I made up, but it works because it honours the three universal truths and it just makes sense.

Step by step, I will share exactly how I do what I do to help you create remarkably fun programs, too. Programs that will leave your group feeling engaged, empowered, valued and meaningfully connected to one another.

Finally, I share ten of the most valuable leadership lessons I have learned that have elevated my facilitation skills from good to excellent.

Part Two: Group Games & Activities

This part is quite possibly the reason you picked up the book. It is jam-packed, full of the best and most fun activity ideas I have come across that require absolutely no equipment.

From the simplest of ice-breakers that will get your group started to a series of complex group problem-solving activities that will challenge your group for an hour or so, here are 150+ outrageously fun and successful no prop activities for you to enjoy.

The activities have been broadly categorised according to their most common use. However, before you dive head-long into the following pages, it is useful to first understand what distinguishes each type of activity from the others.

Group Splitting Strategies

Dozens of inventive, simple and fun ways to split large groups into smaller groups (including pairs) beyond the tired and boring routine of "Okay, pick a partner."

Ice-Breakers & Get-To-Know-You Games

Activities that set the tone, invite people to play, interact and most importantly, laugh. In my opinion, breaking the 'ice' is the most critical (and often least-prepared) part of a program.

Name-Games

Ideas to tempt your group to learn some names. There is no doubt that the higher the level of name-knowingness, the more fun (and trust) your group will develop.

Energisers, Warm-Ups & Stretches

Activities that energise and warm people up, perhaps inviting them to stretch a little – physically, emotionally and mentally. Perfect to let off a little steam, or serve as a quick 'brain-booster.'

Tag & Running Games

This section features games and exercises which are ideal for groups that have plenty of energy to spare or will simply enjoy the wild abandon of a good chase.

Trust-Building Exercises

Activities which are primarily focused on developing trust and strengthening relationships, or that simply embrace the finer moments of being human.

Group Problem-Solving Initiatives

Experiences which are ideal for developing critical interpersonal skills such as communication, collaboration, critical-thinking and creativity. These activities challenge a group to pool their collective resources, solve a problem and then reflect back on what they have achieved and learned.

Fun Community-Building Games

This section features dozens of fun, interactive and engaging activities that will involve your whole group at the same time. Beyond the pure, unadulterated pleasure of mixing and playing, you are sure to discover lots of intrinsic value in these games too.

In all cases, every activity that is shared is enhanced with at least one variation. So, really, you are picking up a vast treasure chest of programming ideas in this book, perfect for any group, especially if you have no props.

Part Three: Resources & Support

The primary purpose of this third and final part of the book is to provide you with a bunch of resources to help you further develop and enhance your skills as a program leader and facilitator.

So as to not clutter the main body of the book, I have purposefully placed a detailed discussion of several key leadership skills here to help you set effective goals, pick the right activity at the right time, and teach safe spotting skills.

Possibly the most powerful and useful section at the back of this book features a description of forty ready-to-play program templates. While there is always the risk of being too prescriptive, there is enormous value in learning from what has worked for me. I expect they will work for you too.

Then, I list a bunch of resources including a free group games app for your smartphone and a series of video tutorials, all of which accompany a suite of professional development options you may find useful.

Finally, if you need help, the final few chapters of the book will give you all of my contact details and a ton of references which point to the science upon which I have relied.

Now, it's time to get started...

part one

POWERFUL
PROGRAM DESIGN

CHAPTER 1
Three Programming Truths

There are a few important things I'd like to share with you before I introduce dozens of wonderful group games and activities that require no equipment whatsoever.

By all means, skip ahead and start flicking through the many ice-breakers, energisers, trust-building and team-based experiences which fill most of this book. You'll find plenty of ideas to inspire you and get your program started.

However, gaining first an understanding of the philosophical framework which is reflected in the description of all of these experiences, not to mention the scientific research which underpins it, will help you squeeze more than just fun from the activities.

Your role, and the approach you adopt is the singular most significant influence on the outcome of your program. That is to say, every time you stand before your group, you have an opportunity to transform their experience from 'That was okay' to 'Wow, that was amazing!' Or not, it's your choice.

There is nothing inherently wrong or bad about leading a series of games and activities without reference to any specific framework or guiding principles. Your group may enjoy a wholly fun and fulfilling time regardless. Or not.

But – please understand this – choosing not to add value (to your group, your program, your leadership skills, etc) is the same as taking it away.

When you consider what is possible for your group and your program outcomes, why overlook an opportunity to squeeze more value? Especially if this experience has the potential to be more fun for more people and can develop critical interpersonal skills at the same time.

What Is Possible?

This is such a powerful question to pose, at the start of any program.

Truly, what IS possible, in terms of what outcome is possible for your group or your program to achieve?

In short, anything you want for your group, right?

But, and it's a *big* but – success in any realm is clearly rooted in the preparation. It doesn't just happen, in the same way that simply throwing a group of people together and expecting them to get along, does not (often) happen.

When I first started as an experiential trainer, I understood the fundamental relationship between what is possible for my group and preparation as a useful 'concept' but I didn't truly understand its critical role in the success of my program.

In the beginning, indeed, the first five years of my career, all I did was emulate the approach of my heroes and heroines in the adventure programming field. In essence, I worked hard to become them.

As a novice, it appeared to me that everything they did turned to gold, so choosing to mimic their approach seemed like a reasonable way to learn. And, for the most part, when I followed their approach, I got similar outstanding results. Fantastic!

But I didn't understand why or how this happened. The intersection between me and what was possible (for my group) remained a mystery.

Approach is everything

As my experience grew, I asked my mentors to articulate why they did what they did, but most of it was explained away as 'intuition.'

Although I was starting to rely on intuition more and more myself, this 'knowing' did little to help others (I was training) understand the art and science of my approach.

Today, after many more years of research and coaching, and certainly thousands of hours of in-the-field experience, I have come to understand three universal truths that support a really powerful approach to programming.

I have referred to these truths in many different ways over the years, and with each re-telling, I refine them just a little to reflect more clearly what I understand works (and what doesn't) to help a group achieve what is possible for them.

Truth #1: Intentionally Build Healthy Relationships

The research is clear (and it makes sense, too) that the most satisfying and successful programs in the world – for the participants and the leader – are those which intentionally promote interaction, build trusting and healthy relationships and take fun seriously right from the start.

Notice, I said 'intentionally' and 'right from the start' – this is no accident.

You see, good outcomes don't just happen, they are created. Simply wishing or hoping something to happen is highly unlikely to achieve the outcome(s) you want. There are many elements which have to be present to produce the desired results. Without these elements, all you have is potential, and potential on its own is not enough to achieve what is (truly) possible for your group.

As I said before, simply throwing a bunch of people together, even with a purpose, does not on its own make a group work. When this occurs – and it does, *a lot* – this is what I've noticed:

- If there's no fun, people find it difficult to engage – with the content or with others;
- If there's no trust, people pull back from participating fully; and
- If there's no challenge, there's only boredom and no opportunity for growth.

The result? Unhappy people, unsatisfactory results and unfulfilled expectations. Un, un, un.

Even programs that specifically aim to address some of these issues come unstuck because they often deliver too much, too little or too late. In other words, these program rarely work because they neglect to embrace what makes us human and that relationships matter.

In other words – approach is everything.

Take, for example, the ubiquitous 'ice-breaker' exercise in which everyone in the room is asked to stand up and introduce themselves, often in the first two minutes of a program. This is a classic case of an excuse of not knowing what else to do.

Programs which intentionally choose to invest the time and effort to build connections (before the content) can expect to amplify the results of whatever they are trying to get done.

Connection Before Content

No matter your curriculum, relationships are key. If you want to inspire and equip your group to achieve what is truly possible, then first, focus on intentionally building trusting and healthy relationships. The stronger and more resilient the relationships in your group, the more productive, more satisfied and more successful your group will be.

When a program fails to focus on the importance of building healthy relationships, you can expect three common problems to manifest:

- You will find it difficult to engage unmotivated or unwilling participants;

- You will lead groups which are unproductive because people don't get along; and
- You will be given too little time to leverage the true potential of your group.

If one or more of these issues strikes a chord with you, then you're in the right place.

If you develop trusting and healthy relationships as an intentional strategy, the research shows that your program will very likely out-perform all other programs on many levels, including greater participation, stronger relationships and increased overall performance.

Now, let's be honest, you want your programs to achieve at least one (if not all) of these results, right?

Yet, a quick glance at many schools today and you could be excused for thinking that the curriculum was all about equipping students for a life of tests, rather than the test of life.

Happily, education systems around the world are beginning to focus on preparing young people for success in life and not just in school. Regurgitating data and following instructions is no longer valued by employers. Rather, they desperately seek people (employees) who can communicate, collaborate, think critically and be creative (the 4 x Cs.)

Skills such as leadership, problem-solving and trust have always been valued, but in an increasingly competitive workplace, these 4 x C skills are the defining features of highly productive and successful groups. And without exception, these skills are intentionally developed in these groups right from the start and not just left to chance.

Presuming this concept of 'connection before content' makes sense to you, let's take the next logical step in this truth-seeking exercise.

Truth #2: Feelings Influence Thoughts & Actions

This universal truth is so simple, yet so rarely understood. How do I know? Just look around – if you meet resistance at any point in your program, then this truth is being overlooked, guaranteed.

It is impossible to change how a person thinks or what they do, unless first, you change how they feel.

This is a fact.

The source of all thinking comes from our feelings, our emotions. Feelings inspire thoughts which equip our actions (our behaviours.) Here are a few examples:

In the middle of the day, you eat lunch because you felt hungry, not because you thought about hunger. At some point in the early afternoon, your body sent a message to your brain that it was time to eat because it experienced a feeling of hunger. You felt a pang of hunger, not thought it. Feelings first.

Or, you are contributing to a group discussion when someone suggests that your strongly-held viewpoint is wrong, and you respond quickly and assertively to defend yourself. Your response is not rooted in your thinking, so much as it was inspired by your feelings of being attacked. You felt vulnerable (this comes first,) then you thought about your response and this manifest itself in your verbal defence of your opinion. This series of events occurs within the space of milli-seconds, but always in this order.

One more. Consider the reasons you chose not to sing a song in front of a group of your peers, many of whom you do not know very well. You're a brilliant singer, but you declined the offer to take the microphone. Not because you couldn't sing, but because you felt embarrassed at the (slim) prospect of failing so publicly. The feelings of inadequacy bubbled up first, which fuelled your thoughts to concoct an excuse (sorry, I have a sore throat,) which supported your actions (remain seated, cast eyes downward, etc) to decline the invitation.

If you have ever met resistance in your program, it is always, always, always because you have failed to focus on the feelings of your group.

It is impossible to change how someone thinks or what they do without, first, changing how they feel.

The only way to influence the thoughts and behaviours of your group is to, first, influence the way they are feeling. This truth speaks directly to the benefits of intentionally building trusting and healthy relationships, because the stronger their relationships, the more willing and able your group will be to think and act in a way consistent with the goals of your program.

It's that simple, but not easy. Our next section explains why...

Truth #3: We Are Comfort-Seeking Machines

The fact that we – human-beings – have survived as a species for so long points directly to the fact that our default position is to always seek comfort. Comfort, or safety, is hard-wired or baked into the DNA of every human-being, so powerful it guides our every feeling, and therefore our thoughts and actions.

This explains the source of our feelings. If we feel threatened, we think and act a certain way. If we feel comfortable, we think and behave in a different way. In short, environment dictates performance.

The logic makes sense, but let's spend a few minutes understanding the science of what's actually happening here (don't worry, it's not too technical.)

Introducing the Zone of Proximal Development

The Zone of Proximal Development (or ZPD) is the name given by psychologists to describe the fascinating process of how people (and therefore, groups) develop their skills. In other words, how we learn, grow and develop as human beings.

The extraordinarily simple, yet powerful model of the ZPD inspires and informs everything about a successful (and powerful) approach to program design and delivery. In short, embracing the technology of the ZPD will help prepare your group for success, ultimately, to achieve what is possible.

Without getting too bogged down in the research and science, the ZPD helps us understand the difference between what a person can do without help (to be successful) and what he or she can do with help. It also distinguishes a zone in which a person can do little other than respond with fight or flight.

These developmental zones, which are just another name for environments, are illustrated and described below.

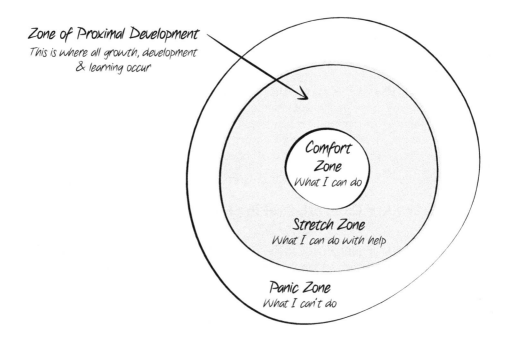

The theory of the ZPD, first developed by psychologist Lev Vygotsky (1896-1934) focused initially on a person's ability to solve a problem. However, over the years, this model has expanded broadly to include the development of all human competencies and skills.

Hence, its relevance to the development of interpersonal skills and the influence your approach has in successfully engaging and attracting your group's willingness to participate.

Comfort Zone

This zone reflects those skills a particular person has mastered, or achieved a level of comfort or satisfaction with. That is to say, the individual does not need any assistance, guidance or tuition to be successful at exercising or performing that skill.

For example, I have a very strong command of the English language. Speaking English fits entirely within my Comfort Zone. However, this was not always the case – consider my ability to speak English when I was two-years old. One of the primary objectives of my school education was to develop my (English) literacy skills, thereby expanding the zone in which I could master (find success with) this skill.

Stretch Zone

The Stretch Zone, or indeed, the Proximal Zone of Development, is the sweet spot of one's education. All learning, growth and development occurs within this zone. Indeed, it is the only zone in which the growth of a human-being occurs. Fact.

By definition, a person may only achieve success in the Stretch Zone with assistance, guidance or tuition. Without this assistance, this person's experience will either push into their Panic Zone (see next section) or retreat quickly to their Comfort Zone.

For example, I can not speak a Chinese language, so when I deliver programs in China I must employ one or more translators to help me communicate my content. Standing before a Chinese-speaking group without a translator will cause me to fail miserably (that is, without a translator, I can not successfully communicate to a Chinese group.) Or, in anticipation of this embarrassing experience, I will retreat to my Comfort Zone and cancel the program.

Or, the decision of a stranger to sit directly next to you on public transport when there were dozens of other empty seats elsewhere in the vehicle. After some initial consternation, some people will not be fussed (Comfort Zone) and happily continue to read their newspaper, while others will shift over a little and perhaps even say hello (an effort which aims to quickly diffuse the stretch and assist the Comfort Zone to expand a little.)

Yet others, faced with this situation, may be pushed beyond the limits of their Stretch Zone into what is called their...

Panic Zone

By inference, the Panic Zone describes those experiences in which an individual can not succeed, because they do not (yet) possess the requisite skills themselves, or the appropriate level of guidance, assistance or tuition is not available to help them be successful. These situations are a step beyond one's Stretch Zone.

When faced with a 'panic' situation, most of us default to one of three scenarios – fight, flight or freeze – none of which are particularly powerful or fun.

We have all felt these moments of 'panic' whether you label them as such or not. Consider the person who suddenly had to manage a stranger sitting right next to them in an otherwise empty public transport vehicle. If this truly reflected a Panic Zone moment, you could forcefully request the stranger to sit elsewhere (fight) or get up and shift to another seat yourself (flight) or remain paralysed with anxiety not knowing what to do next (freeze.)

For the most part, this is an area you do not intentionally or ordinarily want to bring your groups to. The Panic Zone is an extension of the Stretch Zone, but it crosses that nominal line where no learning exists other than perhaps, never to put yourself in this situation again. Rarely productive.

Zone Implications

While simple in nature, there are, however, some important implications you must first consider to broaden your understanding of the ZPD:

- Graphically, it is easy to understand the different degrees to which you can experience comfort, stretch and panic. The closer one gets to the very centre of the circle, the more comfortable (less stretched or panicked) one becomes. And vice versa. Naturally, it always 'depends on the situation.'

- Within a zone, there are varying degrees of comfort, stretch and panic. These also vary among individuals and groups. The challenge, of course, as with all group work, is to design a program which meets the needs of as many people in your group as possible. A neat trick when this happens.

- In short, when given a choice, individuals and groups almost always prefer to operate from within their Comfort Zones, ie that space which is familiar and keeps them safe. This is the domain of routine, boredom and stagnation. People sitting next to people they know. Keeping quiet rather than speaking up and looking foolish. Arriving late because this is easier than accepting responsibility for being on time, and so on.

- Learning, growth and development only ever occur in the Stretch Zone. Clearly then, the primary role of education is to expand one's Comfort Zone by inviting people into their Stretch Zones, frequently. This is the domain of challenge, growth and possibility. People and groups operating within this zone are working hard to realise their full potential. It's not always easy, they often need help, but they achieve so much more.

- The more often people are invited to step willingly into their Stretch Zones, the bigger their Comfort Zones get because they absorb a small part of their old Stretch Zone. In your efforts to create a truly powerful and engaging environment for interaction, this (growing) process should be one of your primary goals.

- Push people too far, and they will enter their Panic Zones and retreat, act out or simply shut down. These are the consequences of not acknowledging people's Comfort Zones (or their feelings) – that is, an environment which is conducive to fun and positive interaction – and expecting anything else will only cause you trouble.

- You must give people a reason to step outside of their Comfort Zones, otherwise, they won't budge. Remember, environment dictates performance. This principle alone explains why many programs meet resistance and fail to achieve their fullest potential. If your group is not ready, they will not be prepared to stretch, yet.

What Does All This Mean?

If you truly want to make a difference – to shift the experience of your program from boring and routine to growth and possibility – you are obliged to invite your group to move out of their Comfort Zones. This shift requires a higher level of interaction, and typically, your group needs your help to do this because they can't (or won't) do it on their own.

Did you get that? Your group needs you to help them.

Unaware that they are stuck, the members of your group are quite comfortable sitting in their Comfort Zones (default human position) so they do not perceive any need for help.

But – and this is extremely important – if they are to consider stepping out of their Comfort Zones, you need to give them a very good reason to do so.

And one of the most powerful reasons is … fun.

As I consider how I do what I do, by far the most potent tool I employ is fun. Fun, taken seriously, is the key. It answers the 'What's in it for me?' question everybody is asking.

Fun is the carrot I dangle in front of people to encourage them to step outside of their Comfort Zones, to experience the value of 'stretching' a little. It is the thread which weaves in and out of my unique approach, a topic we are now ready to explore.

Environment
dictates
performance.

CHAPTER 2

The Answer Is Fun

Or, whatever the question is, fun is the answer.

On many levels, this is true, but we are getting ahead of ourselves.

First, let's recap what we have learned so far, and then connect it to this critical programming element.

This is what we know:

- The most successful programs (think schools, camps, corporate training rooms, sporting teams, families, etc) are those which intentionally develop trusting and healthy relationships from the beginning;

- It is impossible to change how people think or what they do, without first, changing how they feel; and

- Humans are comfort-seeking machines.

In a nutshell, building and strengthening relationships is hard work. Trust does not turn up just because you tell people what to do and how to think. And people are not naturally inclined to want to do this work unless, and until, they are given a reason to do so.

So, the million dollar question is this: If we want people to grow, learn and develop, and we accept that this only occurs in the Stretch Zone, and humans are naturally inclined to seek comfort, how do we influence them to stretch a little?

The most powerful and successful strategy I know is to have fun.

FUNN

Obvious fun is very hard to stand away from. It's contagious and pretty much speaks everyone's language. Fun disarms people, because it often involves a lot of unselfconscious activity. And, let's face it – it's hard to look cool when everyone else is having a great time.

I'm sure you noted the misspelling, but there's no mistake. FUNN is a whimsical acronym which means Functional Understanding Not Necessary, a term coined by the masterful Karl Rohnke that says 'If it's fun, I want to be a part of it.' Which is exactly its purpose.

FUNN is good, agreeable, contagious, its own reward, etc, etc, but it will also help to facilitate your program goals. The best part is that your group does not need to know that this is happening, ie functional understanding is not necessary.

Yet, programmatically, a liberal dose of fun is absolutely essential if you want to influence the way people feel, and create an environment which encourages them to step outside their Comfort Zones.

To this end, fun (no matter how you spell it) is the magnet I use to invite people out of their Comfort Zones to try something new and grow. Think of it as a gentle invitation (a pull towards their Stretch Zone) rather than a coercive push (or a nudge out of one's Comfort Zone) if this metaphor helps.

This Is True, But...

Until now, all of my language has been about inviting people to step out of their Comfort Zone into their Stretch Zone – sorry to say, but this actually isn't happening. Nevertheless, to scaffold your learning, this has been a necessary step in the process of expanding your understanding.

To be fair and scientifically accurate, from the perspective of the participant, they remain most of the time within their Comfort Zone (remember this is our default position.) The 'fun' environment which has developed during the program serves to influence the perception of the task or challenge as suddenly more doable, more successful.

This 'braver' environment causes the participant to stretch themselves (beyond their initial self-perceived limits) which, in effect, expands their original Comfort Zone. And, voila! Call it what you will, you successfully invited this person to grow, and importantly, to do so willingly.

For example, the invitation to stand up in front of a group to introduce oneself in the first two minutes of a program can be a daunting task for some people – an experience well outside one's Comfort Zone for all sorts of reasons. But, to perform this task after several hours of highly-interactive, non-threatening fun which generated lots of sharing, laughter and energy is suddenly a whole lot easier.

Why? Because, it's impossible to change how a person thinks (eg I won't get this right) or what they do (eg I haven't got much to say) without, first, changing how they feel (eg I feel more comfortable or brave now to give this a go.)

One more time – environment dictates performance.

If you create a highly-interactive, supportive and fun environment in which to engage your group, the more powerful, meaningful and rewarding your program will be.

In the next two chapters, I will share the tools and a powerful sequential framework I use to intentionally create this environment.

But for now, it's worth spending a few moments considering the impact of our language, because it informs and guides so much of why this unique approach works.

We All Need Fun To Be Human

I know I have used the word 'fun' to describe the strategy I employ to invite people to step outside their Comfort Zones, but it's not quite the right word.

In purely scientific terms, a more accurate word would be 'flow' but this can be a difficult notion to get your head around, too. Another word that comes close is 'play' but once again, you are likely to misunderstand its true meaning – I'll expand on its meaning for you shortly.

What I can tell you is that the fun I am referring to is one of our most basic psychological needs. As researched by Dr William Glasser, there are four psychological needs of being human:

- **Belonging** – to be loved, to share, to co-operate and be accepted;
- **Personal Power** – ability to achieve, be recognised, respected and feel competent;
- **Personal Freedom** – ability to make choices, to be given responsibility and feel independent; and
- **Fun** – laughing, playing and engaging in healthy relationships.

In essence, this research tells us that incorporating 'fun' into our lives is critical to the healthy and balanced development of being human. As a core psychological need, we may suffer if we do not take fun more seriously.

To my way of thinking, anyone who is responsible for the emotional wellbeing of a group is called to integrate 'fun' (as described by Dr Glasser) into their programs. This means elevating its importance in not only our program approach, but in our discussions with clients in advance of delivery.

Equipped with a growing body of research that fun matters, we can no longer accept the commonly-held notion that fun and play are childish pursuits and a waste of time. To the contrary, and without argument, fun is, and should remain, an integral component of every program. In fact, I would argue that there is no better way to build trusting and healthy relationships.

Importance Of Play

It is no coincidence that many of the characteristics of this psychological need for fun reflect the essential elements of play, as described by Dr Stuart Brown, President of the National Institute for Play. Backed by his research over many years, he has characterised play by seven key properties:

- **Apparently purposeless** – it is enjoyed for its own reward;
- **Voluntary** – people willingly participate, without coercion;
- **Inherent attraction** – something causes you to want to participate;
- **Freedom of time** – you never notice the time passing;
- **Diminished consciousness of self** – you notice little of anything going on around you;
- **Improvisational potential** – there are no rules, little focus on win or lose; and
- **Continuation desire** – you want to keep doing it.

Note, play is not an activity as much as it is a state of mind. It speaks directly to an environment or atmosphere in which participation occurs, which is why a playful approach is so critical to, and successful at creating powerful program outcomes.

Indeed, Dr Brown argues that play is as essential to the development of a human-being as sleep and nutrition.

This is a bold statement, but I whole-heartedly agree. Let's reflect on it for a moment.

To start, I think we can all agree that sleep is fundamentally related to the health of a human-being. Without adequate sleep, we simply do not function as well as we would like. I pushed through three nights without sleep once to complete a university assignment and I was a zombie at the end of it. Consequently, it was not my finest accomplishment.

Equally, there is now solid evidence which clearly shows that eating a balanced, nutritious diet helps us live healthier for longer.

And now, the research is in, suggesting that generous doses of play are as significant to our overall health as sleep and nutrition. Put side by side, this is a very exciting scientific development and happily supports what I have always believed to be true.

Added to this, there is growing evidence which points to a condition called 'play deficit.' It's not causal, but researchers have discovered a high degree of correlation between incarcerated youth and adults and significant deficits of play in their lives, especially their childhoods.

And I know from experience, when groups willingly enter into the space of 'play,' growth and transformation are significantly more possible than without it.

Why? Because, it's impossible to 'pretend' to be something that you are not when you are engaged in play (or flow.)

I don't mean that you can't pretend in the way a four-your old pretends to be super-woman. I mean, it's a lot more difficult to work with a group that is very busy trying to 'be' something that they are not. The sooner those masks are taken off, the better.

Making A Difference

No matter how you describe it, fun or play or flow greases the wheels of interaction and invites people to laugh, share, trust, loosen up, set the tone, change the pace, grow, and so on – all of which contribute manifestly to the breaking of ice and the strengthening of healthy relationships.

Play is as essential to human development as sleep and nutrition.

For example, I always introduce a simple, quick energiser at the very start of a program to engage my audience quickly, and get them laughing and, perhaps, interacting. Sometimes, I connect the exercise to the theme of my session or simply invite everyone to enjoy a moment of play.

Conference organisers and keynote speakers love me for this trick alone. There is nothing better than entering a space which has been warmed up, and exudes a strong sense of everybody leaning in and ready to go.

I have long held the fervent belief that fun group games and activities are a powerful (and attractive) way to help people connect. Having worked with tens of thousands of people all over the world, I know this truth to be self-evident.

I also know that the stronger the connections I build within a group, the more they can amplify the results of whatever they are trying to get done. Greater participation, increased productivity, improved performance, etc, etc.

Which is why you happen to be holding this book, right?

Next, let's discuss four essential tools you can use to intentionally create this environment, every time.

CHAPTER 3

Essential Programming Tools

As discussed, it is impossible to change how people think or what they do without, first, changing how they feel. I shall now describe the tools I use to influence the way people feel.

First and foremost is fun.

As described in the last chapter, it is my most potent tool.

Like detergent, fun has extraordinary power to cut through the dirt. It promotes interaction and frames the use of each of the four other essential tools:

- **Goals** – articulating the difference you want to make and setting clear expectations.
- **Choice** – the ability to choose if, when and how far one may step outside their Comfort Zone.
- **Full Value** – an agreement which frames and adds value to a group's interactions.
- **Reflection** – a process which enables the discovery of learning and growth.

Together, they form the cornerstones of my unique experiential approach to powerful program design and leadership.

The following sections describe each one of these four tools in more detail.

These tools, when used with care and set within a sequential framework (next chapter) create an environment which will help you generate surprising levels of fun and interaction, build trust and leave your group feeling engaged, valued and meaningfully connected to one another.

1. Goal-Setting

The process of setting goals, and working towards them, is very clearly and unquestionably beneficial to your program. It answers the 'Why?' question driving your program.

Research has repeatedly shown that groups achieve more when they set a goal, because goals motivate people as much as guide and direct their energy towards a common objective.

A program goal may sound like... to have fun, to build team skills, to energise and wake up the group, to develop leadership skills, to prepare the group for a certain task, to fill-in time, to open the conference, and so on.

A poor process to setting an effective goal, or worse, the absence of a goal, are two of the main reasons programs fail. In my goal-setting endeavours, I have found it useful to follow the SMART goal guidelines to set effective goals.

Take a look at the resources in Part Three of this book to learn more about setting SMART goals.

Now, having answered the Why? question, this is the point where most program leaders conclude their goal-setting process.

This is a start, and there is nothing wrong with choosing to stop here. You have a goal, and this is better than not having a goal. But, having a goal is not the same as making a difference.

Articulating The Difference

The R of the SMART goal-setting model points to a little of the depth required of this final planning step. It asks the why behind the why.

You can't make a difference without, first, understanding why this difference will matter to your group. Once again, recalling a simple truth – you cannot change how people think or what they do without, first, changing how they feel.

This part of your needs analysis aims to go deeper, to a level which, once tapped, will unlock the true value of your program and more successfully engage your group on their journey with you. This is so important. When you nail this 'difference' you'll be able to identify exactly how you want your group to feel when they leave your program.

There is no set formula, simply an enquiry. There are several tools you can use to drill down deeper, including:

- **The Five Whys** – a simple problem-solving technique that helps you get to the root of a problem quickly. Ask a series of 'Why?' questions with each successive answer to help you understand why your group wants to achieve this particular goal, why this is important to them and to whom does this matter.

- **Empathy Enquiry** – a series of questions which help you understand an experience as viewed through the eyes of your group. It helps you explore why people do what they do, and build empathy for how they think and how they behave. In essence, it explores the purpose, beliefs, values and world-view of your group.

In short, your program will be well served if you can clearly articulate what difference you are going to make. How will this make your group feel, and what do you want them to become?

2. Honouring Choice

None of us enjoy being forced or coerced to do something we don't want to do. Even when these 'things' are good for you, an approach which gives you the power to choose will always be more successful than feeling under pressure to participate because of some threatening external factor, such as your peers, the boss, a teacher, etc.

Remember, you can't change the way people think or behave until you have changed the way they feel. Recognising that authentic change comes from within, this tool creates an environment within which people can feel comfortable to make decisions consistent with, and appropriate to, the overall goals of your program. In short, the ability to choose helps interactions flow.

A term first coined by Karl Rohnke (and later popularised by Project Adventure,) Challenge by Choice is a powerful programming tool which honours people's choice to determine their own level of involvement in any given activity. Nobody is, or should be coerced to do anything that they don't want to do.

Notice then that Challenge by Choice shifts the responsibility onto you, the program provider, to create an environment which encourages your group's participation. Or, in other words, to create a space within which people can step outside their Comfort Zones into their Stretch Zones. This is exactly as it should be, and not the other way around.

Yet, if you take a good look around, you'll discover a disturbingly different picture. I have seen and been a part of too many programs which do nothing to foster a supportive environment, and just expect people to participate. Once again, some program leaders wonder why they meet resistance.

More Than Just Saying 'No'

However, embracing this tool as a core theme of your programming approach is more than simply allowing your participants to say "No" and pull out of an activity.

Honouring choice allows people to pull back from a challenge that may push them into their Panic Zone, and rather than pull out, invites them to find another role (hopefully within their Stretch Zone) that works for them. You could call this a Challenge *of* Choice, whereby someone chooses their level of challenge.

For example, allowing an individual to choose not to be physically carried across the 'peanut-butter' pit as part of a team-building exercise, because they would rather participate in the gentler problem-solving process. Or, instead of addressing the whole class, each student is invited to share their response to the teacher's question with a partner or small group.

When you are profoundly related to this powerful concept of choice, it will permeate every aspect of your program design and delivery. It's the difference between 'You have to...' and 'You are invited to...' Or 'If you make a mistake, you have to come into the centre of the circle...' and '...it's your turn to have some fun in the centre...'

One of your primary responsibilities is to create an environment in which people can make appropriate choices.

Perhaps you already embrace this concept in your program. Fantastic. But note, it's one thing to say '... this program honours your ability to choose your level of participation...'

It's entirely another thing to be responsible for a program that speaks to, honours and fosters an atmosphere in which people genuinely feel comfortable to willingly step outside of their Comfort Zone.

Environment dictates performance. To this end, one of your primary responsibilities as a program leader is to create an environment in which all of the members of your group can make appropriate choices, consistent with the goals of your program.

3. Leveraging Full Value

If honouring choice acknowledges that people tend to enter into a new experience from within their Comfort Zones, creating a 'full value' working agreement is the vehicle that they can use to interact safely and productively within their Stretch Zone.

In the context of preparing powerful spaces within which people can interact, creating a working agreement that values everyone's contribution is all about keeping this space as fun as possible, as much as keeping it as 'safe' as possible.

All people have a right to be valued, and valuing oneself is as important as valuing others. Accordingly, a working agreement creates a coherent, shared and conscious understanding about how people are expected to behave.

To not focus on this critical notion is akin to driving without a seat-belt – the longer the drive, the greater the chance of causing harm in an accident.

You see, the longer people spend together, the more comfortable they become with one another. Slowly, their interactions move into the Stretch Zone, and, it is at this point, we need more than just good intentions to keep things moving smoothly. As with all things in the Stretch Zone, your group will need guidance and assistance.

What Is A Working Agreement?

A working agreement is a device (much like a seat-belt) that helps individuals and groups to achieve their program goals in a safe and supportive environment. No matter what group or program you care to mention – from a weekly youth group meeting to multi-day, team-building workshops – every program will benefit from the process of consciously defining what is expected of people's behaviours.

That said, programs which involve the same people over a long period of time – such as schools, corporate and community organisations – need and benefit from the structure offered by a working agreement significantly more than shorter, one-off programs. Longer programs have more opportunities to develop the hidden potential of the group, and therefore, achieve mightier and more challenging goals.

A working agreement has many and varied forms. It may be written or oral, explicit or implicit, casual or formal. No matter what shape it takes, it is a shared creation, and should embrace three broad tasks:

1. To understand and create safe behavioural norms under which the group will operate;

2. Seek a commitment to adhere to these norms by everyone in the group; and

3. To accept a shared responsibility for the maintenance of the group.

Importantly, the working agreement ought to fit the unique goals, characteristics and spirit of your group. Therefore, the shape of the agreement you develop for a one-hour basketball clinic with children will differ significantly from that created for a residential therapy group for adults. So will the agreement formed between adjudicated youth and that developed for a one-day professional conference.

At one end of the spectrum, the way you lead your program and interact with your group will communicate implicitly what is expected. At the other extreme, you may have to instruct everyone to sign a written contract which explicitly states what is and is not appropriate behaviour.

With clearly defined boundaries, people know where they stand and comfortably make decisions about the type and level of their involvement. The more ambiguous these boundaries are, the less inclined your group will be to interact outside their Comfort Zone.

Why Bother?

Perhaps your group really does care for one another and reflects a wonderfully safe and supportive culture. Maybe. Maybe not.

Most groups, no matter the reason for their existence or length of program, will benefit from some form of 'conversation' which aims to guide their behaviours to, ultimately, leverage their fullest potential. Even groups that have been together for a long time – such as a school class, or a work-team – will gain a lot from the process of sharing and making conscious those aspects of their collective norms that are acceptable, and those that are not.

In my experience, much of the discussion reflects typically unwritten, unspoken laws of 'how we do things around here.' Naturally, for those groups that are just forming, or will only gather for a short time, there is no such thing and will necessarily start with a clean slate.

Even if the list of 'norms' is exactly the same for every member of your group, the process of actually sharing and making this agreement a conscious one benefits everybody. It will set your group up for success, because its potential will not get bogged down in petty grievances and misunderstandings further down the track.

4. Learning Through Reflection

If education or professional development is one of your program goals, this next tool will become one of your most powerful allies.

Experiential-based learning is the process of learning through experience, and is more specifically defined as 'learning through reflection on doing.' That is to say, the practice of simply 'doing' does not, in and of itself, create 'learning.' Reflection makes all the difference.

The term 'learning by doing' is sometimes confused with experiential learning, but they are not the same. A personal example will suffice.

There's one thing most of us learned to do when we were very young. We were told 'once you learn how to do it, you'll never forget.' Riding a bicycle.

And it's true, once you learn how to sit on a bike, pedal and balance all at the same time, you've learned how to ride a bike. Some would argue that this skill is mastered through a process of learning by doing, but they are wrong.

My son learned to ride a bike when he was four years old. After spending almost a year on a 'balance-bike' (regular bike without pedals or training wheels) he was ready to propel himself forward by using the pedals on a slightly bigger bike.

Over the course of a couple of weeks, we would hit the road together. He would work on pushing the pedals and I would help him to balance on his seat. Holding on, I'd walk or jog behind him to keep him upright.

Naturally, there were spills and tears and many days between attempts. Then it happened, he found his balance, and Daddy could no longer keep a hold of the bike. He whizzed away from Daddy, and then after performing a spectacular turn, he sped back towards me exclaiming "Daddy, I got it."

Indeed, he did. Some would argue that he learned (to ride a bike) by doing, but this is scientifically incorrect. He learned to ride a bike by 'not' doing it.

My son learned to ride a bike by discovering all of the ways to not do it successfully, until he did. And with each attempt, assisted by a professional facilitator for a father, my son would reflect back on what went wrong and tried again by doing something different. It was this process of reflection where the true learning occurred. That is experiential learning – a process of learning through reflection on doing.

A Way of Doing

If your program is all about having fun, then a 'hands-off' approach may be fine. But, if you are looking to have a more substantive impact, you are well advised to 'facilitate' the reflection and learning process to benefit your group's development.

Importantly, experiential learning is a way of doing – it is not something that one does. As mentioned, the act of 'doing' does not, in and of itself, create learning. It is critical to facilitate the learning process to ensure your group enjoys more than just fun from the experience. This process, also known as a debrief, review or reflection, is an opportunity for participants to think about what has been learned.

This 'experiential' methodology is ideally suited to the development of key 21st Century skills such as the 4 x Cs of collaboration, critical-thinking, communication and creativity, because these skills can be practiced through a series of carefully sequenced and facilitated experiences.

There is a lot of evidence to suggest that the use of this tool happens most effectively in a four-step process, and adopting this process will help your program – in whole or in part – become a more valuable and meaningful experience for everyone.

The Experiential Learning Cycle (ELC), developed by David Kolb, is an 'action-reflection' model and one of the foundations of adventure education. The ELC will give you a structure to follow in your work as you seek to draw more meaning or learning from your program. It proposes that the transfer of learning will be more effective if what is being learned is discovered though actual experience.

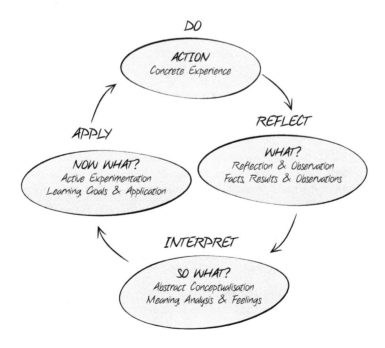

This process, is an opportunity for your group to process what has been learned from a particular experience. Guided by a series of reflective questions which you pose, your group can discuss significant topics and tackle relevant issues, such as communication and leadership within the group. Within the context of a safe and supportive atmosphere (ideally governed by a 'full value' working agreement,) they can also provide feedback to one another and raise valuable learning points.

Obviously, this is higher-order, Stretch Zone stuff. Adopting the action-reflection model of the ELC means that your group can not expect to be fed the answers, so there's work to be done. Starting small and building up over time, you can expect your group to continue to improve, testing the limits of their self-perceived boundaries.

To work effectively, this process works hand-in-hand with each of the other tools, especially when you have articulated the difference you want to make (set goals,) honoured choice and created a full value working agreement.

How To Debrief

As I talk with others, many program leaders feel the least confident or competent in their ability to process an experience compared to their other leadership skills. Fair enough too, because we tend to put a lot of pressure on ourselves to trawl for pearls of wisdom every time we invite our groups to reflect on what they have learned from an experience.

When I think back to my son learning how to ride a 'big-boy's bike,' even a very experienced experiential trainer like myself felt inadequate at times to help my son reflect on what was going wrong.

Happily, volumes have been written about the art and science of reflection skills and they can mostly be summarised into four simple steps:

1. **The Doing** – the action or concrete experience.
2. **What?** – reflecting on the facts of 'what happened' in the experience.
3. **So What?** – generalising these facts, making connections and looking for patterns.
4. **Now What?** – applying this learning to the next experience, or ultimately, to people's real lives – at school, home, work and play.

On one hand, this step-by-step approach points to the science of leading an effective reflection experience, as illustrated in the diagram of the Experiential Learning Cycle. While, on the other hand, the art of reflection is developed slowly, often discovered through trial and error and 'gut' feelings.

One Final Tool

These are the tools I use to help influence the way my group feels, which in turn, influences their thoughts and actions consistent with the difference I am trying to make.

Equipped with this philosophical understanding, you are now ready to explore the step-by-step methodology I use to create the most powerful and rewarding programs possible.

CHAPTER 4

The Difference Model

To be honest, you have most of what you need to know this far into the book to create an outrageously fun, interactive experience which will set your group up for success.

But, there is just one wholly significant element left to describe – the sequence, or the progression of steps to follow to generate success.

Looking back, I wish this sequence, this series of steps, was shared with me when I first started out. For the most part, despite or in spite of my green, dewy-eyed approach, I kind of just figured it out.

I noticed that when I followed a particular sequence, the program worked and my groups left feeling engaged, inspired and successful. Of course, when I did not follow this sequence, I would often fail to achieve my desired outcomes.

Over the years, I have continued to reflect on this sequence. With each book I have written and training workshop I have delivered, I have re-worked it to reflect more accurately how I do what I do. This is what I know works.

To design a program that is fun, engages people and builds and strengthens relationships, I follow these four steps:

1. **Plan** (Articulating Difference) – articulate the difference I am going to make.
2. **Prime** (Setting the Tone) – create a fun & supportive environment to invite interaction.
3. **Pump** (Doing the Work) – develop engagement levels & skills to promote growth.
4. **Peak** (Making an Impact) – leverage my group's potential to do work that matters.

This methodology acknowledges the fact that, by our very nature, people don't like to step outside their Comfort Zones. Consequently, if a program is not fun, or people feel threatened or there's any chance that they will look foolish, the program will fail to achieve its full potential.

In the sections which follow, I describe this powerful four-step framework – which I call the *Difference Model* – in more detail. It will equip you with the skills and strategies you need to prepare your group for success right from the start, ultimately helping you to deliver an extremely powerful program which you and your group will thoroughly enjoy.

This unique approach is not about *being* different, it is focused on *creating* a difference. It appeals to people of all ages, and works with nearly every type of program you can think of.

Step 1: Plan
Articulating Difference

This first critical step is not a guessing game, nor should it be regarded as more important than anything else. But, it does lay a crucial foundation for the success of your program.

Everything about this step points to one critical question: *What difference are you going to make?*

This task is more than just setting goals, it's about clearly identifying what difference your program is going to make in the life of your group, and how it will make them feel? From their perspective.

Often, this is a tough question, because most program leaders think only in terms of goals. Anyone can set goals. Your task is to understand what the real needs of your group are, and to choose a course of action that will make a real difference to them.

A thorough plan, or needs analysis, will involve three steps:

1. Logistics
2. Apparent Goal
3. Difference

Logistics

This first step in the planning process starts with the simple logistics of your program, with answers to six key questions:

- **When** – date, time, scheduled breaks?
- **Who** – number and demographic profile of your group?
- **What** – weekly meeting, annual conference, one-off, urgent, etc?
- **Where** – venue, physical environment, space requirements?
- **How** – form of delivery, eg oral presentation, experiential, online, blended learning?

These questions should not take too long to complete.

The more important work – answering the sixth question **Why** demands more time and effort, and is the focus of the next two steps.

Apparent Goal

There is always an apparent goal – the one staring you and your group in the face. It is often captured in the initial conversation you have (with yourself, or others) when you first consider your group's needs.

Your task here is to set an effective goal, reflecting the useful characteristics of a SMART goal. This is effectively your program objective, and is best expressed in one sentence. Refer to Part Three to learn more about how to write a SMART goal.

As discussed in Chapter 3, having a goal is better than not having a goal. But, having a goal is not necessarily the same as making a difference, which is the domain of the next, most critical planning step.

The Difference

This step expands on the R of the SMART goal-setting model, exploring more deeply the needs of your group, and will identify precisely how the program will leave your group feeling.

An apparent goal is most often expressed in terms of what you, the leader, are trying to achieve. While clearly engaging your group, program goals are focused on *you*, such as 'lead a rock-climbing expedition' or 'present an interactive team-building program.'

In contrast, articulating the difference your program is going to make (for the participants) is more powerfully related to the impact your group is ultimately seeking because it is focused on how it will make *them* feel. For example, to feel valued, empowered and engaged. Or, to feel more confident and in control.

Remember – it's about them, not you. Everything about your program leadership must be viewed through the lens of creating this difference, focused on your group's needs, wants and desires.

To help you, always articulate or express this 'difference' in terms of how it will look, sound and feel.

For example, if the difference I want to create is to leave my group feeling 'inspired and empowered,' I could imagine the following results: my group will look extremely excited to get back to work, they will be heard saying things such as 'I have so many ideas now' and will be bristling with happy, confident feelings.

Here are some questions that will help you explore your group's needs:

- Why does your group want to achieve this goal?
- Why is this important?
- Why does this matter, and to whom?
- Why does your group exist?
- What does your group believe?
- What does your group value?
- What do the people in your group care about?
- What do the people in your group really want?

The more your answers to these questions connect to the feelings of your group, the more successful you and your program will be.

Or, in other words, this is the work of building connections before content.

Practical Planning Considerations

Before we move on, keep in mind the following thoughts:

- First, write your plan down. This simple task puts it into existence and helps you to be accountable.

- Your plan, much like a budget, is a starting point and not a straight jacket. Things will change, so expect to revise your plan as you go.

Ask yourself what difference do you want to make, articulated from your group's perspective.

- Longer programs are sometimes more suited to this needs analysis process. Any process which takes longer than the actual program itself is probably not worth the trouble. That is not to say that short sessions do not benefit, but given the investment of time and effort, articulating a 'difference' may be less useful.

- Be realistic. Ask yourself, what resources do you need to help you make a difference? Are you the best person to lead the program? If not, then who can you involve?

- Write your plan in the positive. For example, 'to help my group feel empowered' rather than 'to eliminate disempowering thoughts and actions.'

- Stress-test your thoughts for making a difference with your group (or group leader.) How do they respond? Does it speak to their issues?

Next, having articulated the difference you want to make, you are now ready to meet your group.

Step 2: Prime
Setting The Tone

This step is the embodiment of connection before content.

Get this step right – it's not hard, but it is critical – and everything which follows will be so much easier and significantly more successful. It's the step most program leaders under-estimate.

This step intentionally creates a fun, safe and supportive environment, where choice is honoured, having fun is paramount and trust is built. All interaction occurs within your group's Comfort Zone, ie that space within which people feel motivated and comfortable to interact with one another.

Ordinarily, this is that part of the program when you pull out your 'ice-breakers,' right?

Wrong.

Guided by the needs analysis you performed in the Plan step, this second step is all about preparing your group – priming them – for the real work ahead.

This step sets the tone and begins the sensitive process of purposefully 'breaking the ice' and switching on people's brains. Recognising their proclivity for starting from within their Comfort Zones, this step is not about playing 'ice-breaker' games as much as it is focused on breaking the ice (as you will learn, these are two very different beasts.)

Involving only experiences which feature fun, simple, non-threatening and success-oriented interaction, here are the four steps which will help you effectively break the ice:

1. Unofficial Start
2. Official Start
3. Small Interaction
4. Bigger Interaction

Breaking The Ice

Having fun and making a difference is not just noticed – it's experienced and felt.

Ask for too much too soon – by not removing the ice – and you'll frighten your group away. But, progress too slowly – by neglecting to focus on your group's potential – and you'll risk boredom setting in.

Naturally, we want to get this right.

To be clear, 'ice' in this context refers to those intangible feelings and beliefs which people reasonably experience that limit or inhibit their interactions with others. Typically, you can expect a lot of ice to be present among people who are new to each other, but it can also manifest itself among people who have known each other for a long time, too.

Little or no talking, poor eye contact, reluctance to make physical contact, lots of standing around, lack of initiative, and an absence of trust or energy are all good examples of ice manifesting itself.

Ice can also look and sound like making excuses, the choice to keep to oneself, arriving late, lying, acting out and looking down at the ground to avoid responsibility.

Basically, any task that requires an individual or a group of people to step outside of their Comfort Zones before they are ready to do so, will trigger a set of feelings, behaviours and survival instincts which result in an icy atmosphere. In short, ice is the devil of group-based programs.

The development of trusting and healthy relationships relies heavily on interaction. Ice prevents this process occurring smoothly and productively, therefore as program leaders we are obliged to remove as much of it as we possibly can. The more ice you break, the more fun and greater the difference you will make in your program.

There are several key elements involved in this step which will help you 'break the ice' and, critically, create a platform upon which your group (and program) will thrive. But, note, this step is not about playing ice-breaker games. It's about introducing experiences that break the ice.

If you or your group cringe at the thought of 'ice-breakers,' then study this step carefully because I'll reveal five reasons why most 'ice-breakers' don't work.

Ice-Breaker v Ice-Maker

Well-versed in the theory that group exercises are a great way to invite people to interact, many program leaders decide to present one or more of these experiences at the start of their program. And then wonder why people sometimes crawl back into their shells.

To truly 'break the ice' and, critically, create a platform upon which your group will thrive, an experience must reflect most, but hopefully all, of the following five criteria:

Fun – the sort of fun I describe in Chapter 2;

Non-Threatening – everything occurs within your group's Comfort Zone;

Highly-Interactive – ample opportunities for people to mix and share with others;

Simple & Easy To Understand – quick and easy explanations; and

Success-Oriented – focus on group accomplishment and worth.

In short, if an activity or experience you are considering does not tick three, four or (hopefully) all five of these attributes, don't do it – it's an ice-maker. Even if you call it an ice-breaker, it won't work well.

An Ice-Breaker?

To illustrate, I need not go any further than contrast this 'ice-breaking' technology with the all-time classic ice-breaker in which everyone in a group is asked to stand up and introduce themselves at the very start of a program.

Nine times out of ten, I guarantee, the program leader will refer to this exercise as their 'ice-breaker.' IT'S NOT. At the very least it's a terrible waste of time, and at it's worst, a horrible excuse for not knowing what else to do.

Now, I'm not saying that you should *never* present this group exercise. That is not my point. My point is, this exercise as described is NOT an ice-breaker, because it does not break the ice.

Let's run through the checklist.

This exercise is rarely fun, except perhaps for the class clown (there's one in every group) who now views the room as a stage, upon which he or she will enjoy being in the spotlight for a moment or three.

Standing up and talking in front of others threatens people. Remember, most people list public-speaking as their number one fear, especially if they have to talk about themselves. This exercise is made even more threatening when the class clown makes everyone laugh, and now it's your turn.

This exercise is not interactive. Most people are too focused on what they are going to say – especially if they're next in line. They are not listening to anyone else. Conduct a survey of how much data is retained the next time you run this exercise, and you'll see what I mean.

Now, to be fair, if there is one thing that this exercise can check off the list, is that the task is relatively simple and easy to understand. It may be simple to understand, but the process it relies on to succeed is very complex indeed.

Finally, being both judge and jury in this case, I think it is safe to say that this exercise is anything but successful. Discomfort and anxiety, not warmth and humour will have started the day. Epic fail.

An experience, any experience, is ONLY ever an ice-breaker when it truly breaks the ice. And this result can only ever be achieved when the experience invites lots of fun, simple, non-threatening and success-oriented interaction.

Okay. Let's move on, and focus on the specific design of the Prime step.

The Four Prime Steps

As with all parts of my approach, there is a sequence involved which makes a difference.

Guided by the five elements I described above, there are four steps I commonly take to set the tone, break the ice and help the members of my group connect more meaningfully with one another.

1. Unofficial Start

Idleness will kill a program, especially if you work with young people. Attract people's attention as soon as possible, and keep them busy. Indeed, I build into all of my programs activities for people to do before the program is scheduled to start – the 'unofficial' start, so to speak.

Unofficial Starts leverage productivity. Waiting is just another word for wasted opportunity. If you take nothing else away from the lessons of this book, this one step alone has the power to transform the results of your program.

The technology of an Unofficial Start helps me manage many situations which most program leaders just put up with (why, I ask?)

Unofficial Starts motivate people to turn up on time, to feel more comfortable, and they generate energy and enthusiasm, and naturally, opportunities to build connections.

To illustrate, I frequently employ the tactic of 'arrival activities,' one or more simple and fun experiences which keep people busy while waiting for the late-comers, gently inviting people into my space. There are always a number of choices, and it never matters if only some of the group actually participate. Generally, those who are busy will generate sufficient energy and buzz, and this activity will attract even more people into the space.

Perfect for conferences, trainings, meetings and events, the Unofficial Start aims to help people feel comfortable immediately – the moment they arrive, whenever that occurs.

This program design imperative features:

- Quick, simple, passive and fun experiences
- Many activity choices
- Immediate attraction and engagement
- Low-supervision
- Low-prop or no-prop

Examples featured in this book include **Paired Shares**, **Imaginary Toss-A-Name Game** and **Tiny Teach**.

2. Official Start

Apart from the obligatory welcome and introduction, I like to keep people moving. You want to keep the momentum going, because if your group sits (or stands) still for too long, you'll lose them.

Official Starts are filled with activities which focus on me (the program leader) – because this is often the safest option, particularly in a room filled with new people – and are imbued with laughter and humour.

To help your group feel welcome and eager to start, choose experiences which feature:

- As few as possible, quick introductions
- Gentle, but fast-paced activity
- Fun as a major component
- Attention focused on you (the leader)
- Creative media

Examples include telling a story to frame the day's program, showing a short video, conducting a walking tour or playing a series of interactive games which introduce key elements of your curriculum.

3. Small Interaction

By small, I particularly mean two (a pair) or three people, and, on occasions, up to eight people. There's no magic in the number – it's just that if you involve too many more, the level of interaction loses some of its intimacy, and people start to feel left out. That's why groups of two people work so well. As I always say, it's hard to be left out of a pair!

This part of your program should involve lots of interaction. In a short space of time, it should be possible for every individual to have partnered, or been in a small team with, most if not all of the people in the group. As an added bonus, invite people to share and capture names as they move about.

This program design imperative aims to help your group feel comfortable and relaxed interacting with others, and features:

- Partner or small group experiences
- Fun as a major component
- Opportunities for sharing
- Emphasis on mixing
- Success-oriented activity

There are too many group activities that involve 'small' interactions to mention, but here are just a few of my favourites described in this book – **Crosstown Connections**, **Cocktail Party** and **Clumps**.

4. Bigger Interaction

Now we move onto larger or (depending on numbers) whole group experiences. Your program builds on the comfort people will have developed working in small groups, and can now expand to embrace higher levels of interaction with more people.

These experiences are designed help your group feel comfortable and relaxed interacting with bigger groups, and feature:

- Large and whole-group activity
- Fun as a major component
- Opportunities for sharing and volunteering
- Emphasis on mixing
- Success-oriented activity

Once again, here are a few of my favourite no-prop style games and activities you can find in this book which involve 'bigger' interaction – **Fill The Space**, **I've Got The Power** and **Fill Me In**.

Practical Prime Considerations

Please note, my discussion and suggestions in this chapter do NOT mean that an ice-breaker has to be a group game or activity.

For example, playing a humorous video as an arrival activity, showing a slide presentation to frame a forthcoming experience, and smiling and shaking the hand of every young person as they enter your drop-in centre, are all wonderful ways to break the ice.

So, when you think 'ice-breaker' think of what 'experience' you could introduce that would effectively break the ice. Some of the tools at your disposal are fun group games and exercises, but you could equally introduce another vehicle or form of media to achieve the same result.

I'm biased, but I happen to believe that ice-breakers which occur in the form of group games and activities are particularly powerful at preparing a group, because they are fun to play and often engage the whole person – body, mind and soul – at the same time.

Given the importance of this critical priming step, here are a few more pointers I hope will guide you to success:

- Avoid elimination games like the plague. I love these types of activities and feature them in many of my programs, but never in the critical priming stage of my group's development. Being eliminated is one thing, but experiencing this over and over and, perhaps, reinforcing what ordinarily goes on for someone (outside of your program,) is stepping into Panic Zone territory.
- One of the most common features of ice-breaking experiences involves the learning of names. My advice – schedule dedicated name-game type activities later into your

program, not earlier. The learning and remembering of names in a social context sits way outside the Comfort Zone of most people. Don't get me wrong – learning names is very important, but there are many, many other ways of capturing names, eg invite people to introduce themselves briefly every time you mix people to form new partners or small teams.

- Keep in mind, while infinitely malleable, resisting change (stepping into the Stretch Zone) is baked into our DNA as human beings. We're open to change, but we need to adjust to the prospect slowly, if possible. To this end, go easy on your group. In my experience, while most groups are willing to embrace change, they sometimes just need a little more time and preparation to get there. The more you can respond to their question 'What's in it for me?' the sooner they will arrive. That's why giving people a choice and making it fun is so important.

Only experiences which invite lots of fun, simple, non-threatening forms of interaction will help you break the ice.

- To help you make decisions regarding the actual sequence of your activities, refer to the GRABBSS model in Part Three of this book. It's a simple and effective assessment tool that you can use to help choose experiences which are appropriate for the unique characteristics and skills of your group.

- You may be wondering how long each of the sequenced steps of the four ice-breaking stages last. This is too difficult to answer because every group and program is different. But, I will say this – you should continue to break the ice for as long as it takes. Anything sooner, and you'll stunt what is possible for your group.

Step 3: Pump
Doing the Work

The first two steps – Plan and Prime – will have worked their magic to have prepared your group as much as possible. It is difficult to under-estimate their power to set your group up for success, helping them connect more meaningfully with one another.

Yet, jump to this third step in the sequential framework too early (which many program leaders do) and you can expect trouble. The sort of trouble that occurs when people are pushed outside of their Comfort Zones and do not want to be there. Your efforts to appropriately and sensitively set the tone and break the ice instantly changes this awkward landscape.

Now, feeling switched on and excited, this third step will uncover your group's hidden potential. It's not rocket science, but the work involved subscribes to the common understanding that the more you train and flex your muscles, the stronger you will get.

In essence, this step asks the question we started with – what is possible? Do the work, pump like crazy, and you can expect more fun, more leverage, more value – in this order.

Content Is King

In practice, this third step of *The Difference Model* is focused primarily on your program, your curriculum, the reason it exists.

No one attends a conference, or a training session or a residential camp just to learn names and play games. People participate in these programs for a specific purpose – a purpose, admittedly, that can be magnified when governed by a powerful program design – but they do not consciously turn up because of this approach.

Approach is important, but content is king. Don't forget that.

Adapting what George Leonard said when he was referring to competition, 'Like a little salt, it adds zest to the game of life. But when the seasoning is mistaken for the substance, only sickness can follow.'

Do not mistake this (or any) approach for the substance of your program – it is simply a tool, a way to deliver your content, to make a difference.

If you're a basketball coach, the reason young people turn up at your class is to learn how to play basketball as a team. If you're running a conference, the reason delegates register for your program is to network and develop their professional skills.

There are any number of reasons why people attend your programs. Over time, one of them may be that you become known for making a difference, and exceeding people's expectations. But, the essence of your program will and must always be the reason for your program. And then, the manner in which you lead it will determine how much of a difference you can make.

The simple argument of adopting the sequential framework of *The Difference Model* is that your program is going to be delivered anyway – why not have fun, engage people and build and strengthen relationships along the way? In short, make a difference.

Critical Interpersonal Skills

Content is your domain. If you have invested adequate time and effort to prepare your group for the work ahead of them, they will be ready to step outside their Comfort Zone and stretch a little.

Remember, all activity within one's Comfort Zone requires no assistance because, for the most part, people can experience success without it. This third step deliberately invites your group into their Stretch Zone, and therefore, by definition, requires the development of trust and your guidance to be successful.

From a leadership perspective, your most critical 'pumping' role will be to help your group create and maintain a safe, supportive and fun environment within which to function and grow. This space, if crafted intentionally, will build trust and strengthen the relationships of your group, all of which stimulates growth, ie an expanding of one's Comfort Zone.

Four of the most useful skills to help you leverage this growth are the four C's –

1. Communication
2. Collaboration
3. Critical-Thinking
4. Creativity

In recent years, many publications and many more topics of research have explored the importance of developing a range of key skills which equip individuals and groups for success in the 21st Century.

These skills focus on more than just filling our heads with knowledge of specific content areas. The research argues that the acquisition of these key skills can be applied to all areas of our lives, not just at school or a specific job.

Fully acknowledging that connection comes before content, this step intentionally builds and strengthens trusting and healthy relationships, the bedrock of individual and group success.

A further focus on the development of the 4 x Cs will not only help your group safely navigate their Stretch Zone, but set them up for success in everything they do.

The following sections explore each of these four skills in more detail, with a number of suggestions and activities to help you intentionally develop these skills within your program.

To assist with your planning, every activity described in this book has been listed under one of these four key skills in the Index.

1. Communication

Expressing thoughts clearly in written and oral forms, articulating coherent instructions and opinions, listening effectively and motivating others through powerful speech have always been highly-valued skills.

 In the 21st century, these communication skills are considered more important than ever.

There is an overwhelming volume of communication in our lives today. Individuals and groups need to be able to determine which sources are accurate and which are not. Fluent reading, writing and speaking skills are essential too, especially in an ever-expanding global marketplace in which technology is leveraging relationships that span multiple time zones, cultures and languages.

There has never been a group I have worked with that did not benefit from improving this essential skill. The more effective an individual or a group communicates, the more success they will achieve.

Experiences which develop communication skills provide an opportunity for people to share their thoughts, feelings, intentions and behaviours more effectively.

Here is a short list of experiences which focus on the development of communication skills, which occur in almost all types of programs, including:

- Practising the art and science of 'active' listening.
- Participating in an exercise or project which requires the group to reach consensus.
- Taking turns to lead the weekly meeting.
- Repeating back what someone just said to explore comprehension.
- Giving and receiving constructive feedback to an individual or group.

Activities you can find in this book which focus specifically on the development of effective communication skills include **Mute Line-Up**, **Charade Line**, **Body English** and **Identity Crisis.**

2. Collaboration

Working together to achieve a common goal has always been useful, but in our inter-connected world, it is essential to the accomplishment of almost all significant work today.

For example, consider the collaborative culture of Wikipedia, which has clearly demonstrated how people working together can produce highly valuable and inclusive results.

Collaboration leverages the synergistic elements of diverse groups of people, where the group is often smarter than the most intelligent person in the team. Working collaboratively also brings multiple perspectives to bear on a group's problem-solving and decision-making processes.

Collaborative efforts not only create more holistic results, but this work creates access to more information, expertise and skills than any one individual can bring.

Yet, as complex and dynamic beings, it can also be very hard for some people to focus on the benefits of collaboration instead of the rewards of individual effort and competition. This is Stretch Zone work, and therefore, requires careful and well-timed facilitation to help your group focus on the benefits of working together effectively.

Once again, there are many practical examples of how you can develop collaborative efforts in your program:

- Inviting two or more people to co-author an article, report or presentation.
- Team up with experts from multiple disciplines to lead a long-term project.
- Ensure that everyone has been consulted for their opinion before a decision is made.
- Seeking feedback from your peers to help you continuously improve.

Activities in this book which focus specifically on the benefits of working collaboratively include **Blob Tag**, **Everybody Up**, **Group Compass Walk** and **Span The Room.**

3. Critical-Thinking

The link between critical-thinking and one's education is obvious – you can't learn well unless you think well.

Critical-thinking is the ability to look at problems in new ways, to analyse how parts of a whole interact with one another and to interpret information and draw conclusions.

Critical-thinking and problem-solving skills were once thought to be the domain of gifted people. Today, they are necessary for every individual and group who seeks to make sensible decisions about financial, health, civic, workplace and leisure activities.

For example, the solutions to international concerns such as climate change and global warming require highly developed critical-thinking and problem-solving abilities. These skills include the ability to effectively analyse and evaluate evidence, arguments, claims and beliefs.

The ability to solve interesting and unfamiliar problems often leads to the development of other skills such as increased engagement, higher concentration levels and improved thought processing.

Here are a few examples of experiences that occur in many programs which may provide you with an opportunity to focus on problem-solving skills:

- Forming a project team to solve an existing, yet complex problem.
- Thinking of a new campaign slogan to broadcast a difficult, yet important message.
- Adopting a rational, analytical and evidence-based approach to investigate a conflict.
- Challenging one of your group's long-held beliefs or practices.

Activities you can find in this book which may help you develop the critical-thinking and problem-solving abilities of your group include **Come To My Party**, **Magic Shoes**, **Spectrums** and **This Or That**.

4. Creativity

Creativity and innovation are key drivers of the global economy. In today's highly competitive and automated world, a creative spirit and the capacity to innovate are fast becoming pre-requisites of personal and professional success.

Creativity is a way of living, and makes life infinitely more interesting and fulfilling. Creative people invent, imagine, problem-solve and communicate in fresh new ways.

The seeds of creativity live in everyone, but some individuals are more fortunate than others because their imagination has been nurtured and grown to become strong personal traits. It is fair to say that groups which fail to create and innovate will be under-prepared for the challenges of tomorrow.

It's more than just thinking outside the box. Creativity demands vision, persuasion and wisdom. Once again, this is the realm of one's Stretch Zone and requires your timely and thoughtful facilitation to stimulate the creative energies of your group.

Opportunities to embrace a creative mind-set may occur in many places in your program including:

- Viewing all challenges as opportunities for growth, eg failure as a platform for success.
- Using a wide range of creative techniques to generate new ideas, eg brainstorming, Edward de Bono's Six Thinking Hats technology, etc.
- Truly listening to new ideas and/or those you disagree with.
- Spending time alone, to contemplate and recharge.

Activities in this book which may help your group develop creativity and innovation skills include **Funny Walk**, **Popsicle Push-Up**, **Spot The Difference** and **The Story Game**.

Practical Pump Considerations

Here are a few things to note in your spare time as a facilitator of growth:

- Having exercised their muscles stepping into their Stretch Zones, help your group to understand that sometimes this process will hurt a little. Growth always involves some form of pain, and this is true for group development, too.
- Expanding on the last point, this is the reason that this step in the programming model is more valuable for longer-term programs, eg school classrooms, corporate teams, residential camps, etc. When things get a little sticky, there is always time for the group to sort itself out, learn from the experience and move on.
- Given the dynamic nature of human beings, there is no hard-and-fast rule that says one experience or activity develops one particular skill more than another. The beauty of much of this work, especially if you utilise group games and activities, is that most experiences can be designed for a wide range of uses. For example, the activity **Mute Line-Up** can be an ice-breaker, an energiser and a problem-solving activity. The critical ingredient will be your primary objective for introducing this experience and your framing of the activity as part of your overall sequence.
- Once again, to help you make decisions regarding the actual sequence of your activities, refer to the GRABBSS model in Part Three of this book. In particular, study the discussion about the sequence of stages in which groups develop, as it applies to your group.

If you have planned, primed and pumped like crazy, then your group will be ready to peak.

Step 4: Peak
Making An Impact

This final step in your program is the opportunity to see the difference you've been looking for.

If you have planned, primed and pumped like crazy, then your group will be seriously ready to peak. Working well together, having fun and feeling connected, you and your group now have the opportunity to make an impact.

It's time to lead.

Run that weekly youth group meeting, teach that swim class or math lesson, hold that conference, deliver that staff training program, conduct that bush-walk or first-aid training course, and so on.

From a classroom to a corporate training room, or a conference auditorium to a weekly youth group meeting, the more effort and time you invest in creating a safe, supportive and fun environment for your group, especially early on, the more powerful and rewarding your program will be.

As already discussed, those programs which intentionally develop healthy and trusting relationships out-perform all other programs on so many levels, including greater participation, stronger communities and increased overall performance.

But, really, the most rewarding outcomes are experienced in the way your program leaves people feeling. Engaged, empowered, valued and meaningfully connected to others are all wonderfully inspiring outcomes.

Practical Peak Considerations

Follow a plan, use the tools available to you, and do everything you can to prepare your group to give them the best chance of not only getting what they came for, but so much more.

Finally, a couple of thoughts to consider before we get into the more practical sections of this book:

- Keep it fun and have fun. Take fun more seriously. It's the reason I'm still in this game after so many years, and it's the reason people keep coming back.
- *The Difference Model* is not a 'set and forget' mechanism. You need to keep working at it, keep choosing to make a difference every minute of the day. There will be ups and downs, and there are no guarantees. It is not the answer to everything that keeps you up at night. That said, I am hard-pressed to find a situation in which this approach to programming does not have a positive impact.
- Finally, I fervently believe that program leaders, whatever variety, lead best when they forget about themselves and focus on their group, their needs and their goals. To lead is to serve, to give, to achieve together.

CHAPTER 5

Top Ten Strategies For Success

Many years ago, I started to record a list of all the activities I had been exposed to – mostly as a participant – during my early training experiences.

Reflecting my fastidious inclinations, I grouped similar activities together, so that as the list grew longer and longer, I would find it easier to access them when I needed a good idea. Ice-breakers, de-inhibitizers, warm-ups, initiatives, trust exercises, games – I recorded the names of everything.

Thirty years later, that list has grown into what I refer to now as my 'Book of Tricks.' There are simply hundreds of great activity ideas contained between its seriously dog-eared covers.

Yet, as much as this book represents a chronicle of what I have played and discovered over the years – and continue to draw benefit from – it would fail to inform even the most learned of my colleagues the slightest glimpse of what I have discovered along the way.

And, most importantly, it fails to offer a glimpse of what I believe to be more significant than the games themselves.

As I flick through its pages, I know for a fact that my briefing, presentation and understanding of many of the earliest recorded activities has changed significantly – for the better – since I first learned to play them.

It's true, I have added many new and wonderful variations to my list of games, but this is not the difference I speak of. Rather, I refer to the philosophies and general comprehension of how play can develop positive relationships that now envelops my facilitation style and overall program delivery approach.

As an experiential trainer and author with 30+ years experience, I often muse about these differences for the benefit of my training participants.

Now, in no particular order, I think it's time to write them down.

Visit **playmeo.com/facilitatortips** for dozens more facilitation tips and strategies, all supported with a video tutorial.

1. Frame, Frame, Frame

In other words, prepare, prepare, prepare.

Appropriately framing an activity – that is, to 'set the scene' or provide a context in which the activity will take place – is one of the most valuable tools I employ to help groups achieve their goals, ie get success. Otherwise, your group may not be ready – in most cases, emotionally under-prepared – for what is about to happen.

People have a natural proclivity to want to know why they are doing what they are doing. Framing goes a long way towards answering these questions, as well as reducing anxiety, providing clarity, and generally coaxing people forward into your program, perchance, into their Stretch Zone.

Everything you do programmatically provides the context in which the next activity is framed. For example:

- Your language – it's not just what you say, but how you say it – see the next tip for a more thorough discussion;

- Lead-up activities – like building blocks, every activity should aim to complement the next, rather than subvert it. To illustrate, leading into a serious discussion after a very energetic, bounce-off-the-wall type of activity is unlikely to result in a settled, composed or focused group of people.

- Your general approach to facilitation – if you operate under the premise of 'challenge by choice' but your overall demeanour limits people's opportunity to make choices, you are likely to turn them off.

Ask yourself, 'Have I done everything to prepare my group – emotionally and physically – to experience success?' and 'Do they know what they are getting into, and why?'

If not, think about what lead-up activities you could use to prepare them, or perhaps what introduction or briefing might be necessary to soothe the group into the activity.

2. It's All In How You Say It

As a participant, which would you prefer to hear?

'....and if you're too slow, or get the wrong answer, you are 'out' and you have to come in to the centre of the circle…'

Or, '…and if the time expires, or you make a mistake, you are invited to take your turn in the centre of the circle and have some fun…'

Perhaps each statement is saying the same thing, but for many people, they will hear a big difference.

The first implies that I have no choice ('you have to') so I might feel under pressure because I don't want to be 'slow' or 'wrong.' This may manifest itself as, I don't want to make a mistake, so perhaps I won't play.

While the second statement is all about options (you may decline the invitation) and fun is introduced as an integral part of the consequence of 'going out.'

As program providers, our language is one of our most potent tools. It can work for us or against us, and I don't just mean the use of 'politically correct' terms. Beware that everything you say, from the moment you introduce yourself to the waves good-bye at the end, will fan the flames of invitation and play or snuff them out.

Ask yourself, 'Have I introduced this activity in the most appealing, inclusive way?' Provide choices to people so that they can find a level of participation that is comfortable for them.

3. Inject Lots Of Humour

This is such a critical element of my delivery, and to be honest, the trick to disarming my group.

Take time to observe the crazy, menial little things people do, and serve it back to them in a manner that asks have you ever noticed this? Of course they have, they just don't want to admit it.

For example, the insistence some people have for tagging their opponent after you have stopped the game, or the understated crawling on knees when a simple pivot on one knee was sanctioned.

Or, at a more serious level, the subtle glance over the shoulder to check that your spotters really are there behind you to catch your fall, even though the command 'Ready, fall away' was given.

What about the way we (notice, I'm using the royal 'we' here, so as to not draw attention to myself) divert our eyes and attention away from someone whom we met and learned their name earlier in the day, but now that they are coming our way, can not for all the fish in the sea remember it? I could go on and on....

Suffice to say, people love to laugh at these silly interactions – it was the essence of the TV show 'Seinfeld.' Our programs are made up of so much normalness, perhaps nothingness, it can be hilarious to sit back and look at it for what it really is at times.

Of course, how you deliver these moments is important – what could appear to some as a diamond in the rough, may just be a rock to others. Focus your humour so that you encourage your group to laugh *with* rather than *at* others.

Oh, and inject tons of FUNN too – it will act as a magnet for many more moments of people simply being human!

4. Let The Group Create Its Own Energy

Or, put another way, if you build it, they don't always come.

Having just encouraged you to inject lots of humour, I have to admit, that some groups just don't get it. You can lay out the most fun, most inviting program ever, and yet, they still won't laugh.

In the early days, my typical reaction to this scenario was to work even harder, and generate the energy myself that I expected to come from my group. After 'hitting the wall' and exhausting myself on several occasions, I finally got it.

Give yourself and your group permission to discover their own energy. It will be different for every group, and provided you have created a caring and supportive environment within which to play, wherever the group is at is where the group is supposed to be. End of story.

Sure, pepper your program with a little more FUNN, add a little levity, but do not generate the energy for your group based solely on your own efforts. You will burn yourself out, quickly. And importantly, you will cheat (ie disempower) your group the opportunity of being the cause of it's own outcomes.

5. How To Pick A Partner

Have you ever noticed how the seemingly innocuous words 'Okay, everybody pick a partner....' can strike fear into the hearts of many participants? In my experience, it is one of the most frightening things you can ask a group to do.

Questions such as 'Should I pick someone, or wait to be picked?' or 'What if I pick somebody, and they don't want to play with me?' or 'Does she really want to play with me, or is she just being nice' or 'If I pick him, will he think I'm hitting on him?' will be roused among many others.

Sadly, the instruction to 'pick a partner' is too-often interpreted as 'find someone you like or are like.'

This thought is as embarrassing as it is open to the anxiety-laden prospect of people feeling left out. There are just too many other ways to ask people to form into smaller groups, including pairs, to risk these outcomes.

Now, I'm not suggesting that you should never use the words 'pick a partner' again. Certainly, as your program develops and your group becomes more comfortable with each other, the panic-inducing reaction to simply 'picking a partner' will diminish.

But, with most groups, especially if they have just met each other, you are well advised to avoid the typical 'pick a partner' suggestion.

Take a look at the Group-Splitting Ideas in Chapter 7 for dozens of fun, often random methods to help you break your group into partners and small teams.

6. Always Ask For A Volunteer

There is always, no matter how long you wait, someone willing to step forward as a volunteer, and help you do whatever you need to do. Perhaps you need help to demonstrate the next move, or need someone to break the ice and start the activity, whatever. It never fails, there is always someone willing to step forward.

But why bother, you may ask, when you can often save time and potential embarrassment by doing it yourself, or asking a colleague to step in? The value is hidden in the invitation.

It can be as simple as observing the initial humour of no-one stepping forward, or everyone but one poor soul stepping back. However, beyond the humour of these moments, there is extraordinary value enlisting the support of a volunteer from your group.

Having one or more of your group step forward says 'I am willing to… take a risk, have fun, give it a go, look silly, etc, etc.' These are huge transformative messages that are broadcast loud and clear – yet subtly – to the rest of your group. It will frequently open up further opportunities for more of these decisions, from more of your group.

Asking for volunteers is part of the fun, it's suspenseful ('what are they going to do?') and it's a true adventure, especially if you don't telegraph what you are going to be doing in advance.

Besides, I get to be up-front all the time, I want to share the limelight from time to time.

7. Have More Up Your Sleeve Than You Need

You can never have too many activities lined-up in your head, nor too much equipment at the ready. This could be just another way of saying 'be prepared,' but it's more than that. It's about options.

Stuff happens – the bus arrives late, it starts to rain, the room is smaller than you anticipated, a member of your group is nursing an injury or disability, etc, etc – all of these events call for immediate attention.

Your example will inspire your group to have fun & take risks too.

Sometimes, it may be just as simple as getting to the end of your list, and realising too late that the activities ran for much less time than you had imagined.

I can't tell you the number of times I have been 'saved' from that menacing what-are-we-going-to-do-now look by resorting to Plan B, C or D, and making it look like I had it all planned from the start. It's always better to say 'Gee, I didn't get to do half of what I planned...' than 'Arghhhh, I need to think of something quick...' It makes you look good too!

8. Stop An Activity Before It Wanes

Always leave your group wanting more.

Stopping an activity just as it reaches its peak, and perhaps a tad further, will give you many useful programmatic starting points.

Moving on at this juncture keeps the energy of the group and their spirits high. It's easier to slide into the next activity if you have their attention, even if they are complaining that you stopped too soon. Better this, than having no complaints because everyone left the scene on account of boredom!

You can always go back to the activity if it really is that good (and it fits your program goals,) but it's often better to move onto something new while you have them in the palm of your hand.

And remember, quoting the evangelical words of Karl Rohnke, if at the end of the day you have waned more often than you waxed, get a new job.

9. Try New Things All The Time

It's easy to fall into the pattern of doing the same old thing, for no other reason than it works. And that's okay, but... there's a lot to be said for trying out new stuff too.

Indeed, seek out new ideas and experiences. Experiment with some new activities, or change the prop or the scenario, even the reason for doing it – just because you can.

I'll even use an activity I don't like much and haven't used in years, just to see if my suspicions hold true. Sometimes they do, but not always – and that's the key. You'll never grow in terms of your confidence, your repertoire and your experience unless you give 'new' a go.

Your Comfort Zone as a leader will stretch too, which is what many of our programs are about, right?

Which brings me to my next pearl of programmatic wisdom...

10. Walk Your Talk

Example is a powerful cause in people's life. If your group sees you do the very thing you are asking them to do, they are more likely to do it too. This is one of the primary reasons I love my work, because I get to play and join in on the fun, rather than stand back all the time.

But more than just participating, walking your talk embraces everything about your program and who you are to your group – from the language you use and encourage, to the choices you make and respect – it all matters.

If you can mix it with your group (when it is appropriate) and demonstrate that you are prepared to take risks (for example, in the challenges you set, and the types of activities you use,) your example will inspire your group to have fun and take risks too.

Naturally, there are times when you need to step back and let your group play and learn on their own. However, please acknowledge that some groups like nothing more than to see their teacher, leader, coach, whomever, do the activity with them.

One further nudge – I surmise that about 95% of the activities I know and deliver I have learned through direct experience. Be it as a participant of someone else's program, or an activity that I've just picked up from somewhere (ie a book or a peer,) almost all of the activities I know and present I have done as a participant.

I also strongly believe that this experience of being a participant – as distinct from being the leader – will make you a much better facilitator of the activity. Actual get-your-hands-dirty participation will give you direct knowledge of what it feels like to be a participant in the activity – which no book or learned colleague's stories about a new, you-beaut activity could ever substitute. It will also keep you fresh, you know, in a way that reminds you what it's like to be a participant again.

And if all of this has failed to impress you to walk your talk, just do it because it's fun.

Now, as you can see below, there are still more top tips to describe.

I promised to share ten of my top strategies for success, but there is just so much to share. Here are three more, must-have leadership strategies you need to know...

11. Play On

Have you ever been left out of a group? Ever felt that everyone else was having fun, but you weren't?

You're not on your own – I've been there, and done that, especially when I was younger. So I make it a point not to introduce too many activities that eliminate people, especially early in a program.

Games which eliminate folks can be great fun – I still use many of them in my programs today. For example, take a look at **Ah So Ko**, **Speed Rabbit** and **King Frog**.

But... when used at the wrong time, or in the initial stages of a group's development, elimination games risk alienating certain people, not to mention, losing a lot of useful energy.

Also, it is not unusual to watch the same people get eliminated over and over again. Beware what message this may send to your group – and those unlucky individuals – if this does not occur within a safe and supportive environment.

If you must (or want to) present an elimination-style activity, look for ways to actively engage those who are eliminated in a new role, such as a heckler, time-keeper, etc, to add more fun and value to the exercise.

Clearly, the more people you have involved, the more energy and good times you can develop – which brings me to my next point.

12. Keep People Bunched Together

The wall-flower syndrome – you know, those folks who like to stand away from the group with their backs to the wall – is such a killer of energy and enthusiasm, especially in the beginning stages of your program.

Always invite people to come closer to you, get them to bunch up a little. Circles work fine, but when you don't need a circle, collapse them in, and ask people to move closer to you. You and they will bristle with energy, which is a wonderful way to build interest in what you're about to share.

My style is very much 'Hey, come over here, I've got a secret to tell.' People move in, they lean closer, their attention is piqued. I love that. They are now primed, and ready to rock-n-roll. Yet, at the same time, my group has started to unconsciously break down some barriers, not to mention, trust and share a little too.

Try speaking a little softer, that often works a treat. Your group will have to bunch in closer to simply hear you. And all those folks who can't hear you because they are too busy talking, will suddenly gasp when they realise the group has gone quiet! I love the humour these moments bring.

Oh, there is just one caveat – never ask a very large group of over-enthusiastic children standing in a circle, to take a few steps into the centre towards you – before you know it, you will be under the biggest pile of 'stacks on the mill' you've ever had the back-breaking pleasure to be a part of.

13. Seek Feedback All The Time

Finally, if you are keen to improve your leadership skills, one of the best things you can do for yourself is to seek feedback. And the best time to do this is when you don't want to hear the answers.

Yes, you read that correctly. It is often the things we don't want to hear that provide wonderful opportunities to step outside of our Comfort Zones to help us continuously improve our leadership skills.

Seek feedback from your peers and colleagues in particular. Sure, you can ask your participants and program clients for feedback, but their opinion will rarely go beyond the standard 'Oh, that was really good' or 'That sucked' remarks.

Discussing your progress with someone who knows what it takes to be an outstanding program provider will inspire greater insight and a more meaningful response. Comments such as 'Your assessment of the group's skills at X point was brilliant' or 'Try to ask simple questions at the beginning of your debrief' are good examples of specific, constructive feedback.

It's not always possible, but try to work alongside other colleagues as often as your program and/or budget will allow. Sharing the lead with one or more people can be a lot of fun, and will provide you with a number of perspectives from which to receive pointers, advice and praise.

part two

GROUP GAMES
& ACTIVITIES

CHAPTER 6
Activity Framework

1. Categories

The activities herein have been broadly categorised according to their most common use.

However, before you start browsing the hundreds of ideas I have shared, it is useful to first understand what distinguishes each type of activity from another.

Group Splitting Strategies

Dozens of fun, random ways to split larger groups into smaller groups.

Ice-Breakers & Get-To-Know-You Games

Activities that set the tone, invite people to play, interact and laugh.

Name-Games

Ideas to help the members of your group learn new names.

Energisers, Warm-Ups & Stretches

Activities to fill-in time, energise and warm-up your group.

Tag & Running Games

Games and exercises to cause your group to run around and let off steam.

Trust-Building Exercises

Activities to develop trust and strengthen relationships.

Group Problem-Solving Initiatives

Activities to develop critical interpersonal skills such as the 4 x Cs.

Fun Community-Building Games

Tons of interactive, engaging, large-group activities that are just fun to play.

2. Format

A brief statement will follow the name of each activity to describe the essential elements of the experience. Every activity will then be described, for the most part, using the following attributes:

Benefits

List of the primary outcomes you can expect to gain from this activity, including one or more of the 4 x Cs – communication, collaboration, critical-thinking and creativity.

People

Recommended number of participants the activity is best suited for. If necessary, minimum and maximum numbers will be expressed.

Time

Number of minutes (within a range) you can expect the activity to run, not including the briefing, or variations.

Instructions

Step-by-step instructions to help you present the activity clearly and successfully.

Variations

Brief description of one or two popular variations of the basic activity, featuring simple rule changes to more complex parameters.

Reflection

Series of questions you can use to reflect on some of the most common teachable moments your group may experience in the activity.

QR Code

Use your smart phone to scan a unique digital code to access exclusive online resources about the activity, such as videos, leadership tips, variations and program templates.

As they say, a picture tells a thousand words. Accordingly, each activity will also be accompanied by an illustration which aims to capture the 'magic' or critical elements of the experience.

3. Tweaking The Challenge

This book presents only a common description of each game, followed by at least one or two variations, so you may think that this is the only way to present the activity.

Another trap is to believe that because an activity is listed under one category (eg icebreaker) that it can not be used elsewhere in your program sequence (eg a group initiative.)

Neither of these two presumptions is true.

First, the beauty of almost all of the activities described within these pages is that they can be varied in many different ways. For example, consider **Freeze Frame**.

This activity is typically used to get people moving and interacting in a defined space. But, with a few rule changes, it can provide wonderful insights into how well a group is connected to one another.

As a second example, consider **Mute Line-Up**, a classic group-based initiative that is perfect for learning about communication skills. But, with less emphasis on how people find their spot in the line, it is a fantastic and speedy method of forming a straight line.

One of the surest ways of transforming an activity from, say an ice-breaker to a trust exercise or a group problem-solving exercise to a tag game, is to adjust the challenge. Or, within the context of an initiative, you may simply wish to make it easier or harder for a particular group.

Here are a number of variables you can use to adjust the challenge of an activity, or to help you deal with that dreaded 'I've-done-this-before' syndrome. Some of these ideas come under the general heading of 'rules,' but some are required during the briefing of your activity.

Time
Introduce a time limit to reflect stress and real world deadlines, or remove one to assess how well the group copes with open-time lines.

Resources / Equipment / Space
Supply more or less resources to your group such as information, equipment, technology and even physical space.

Handicaps
Removing the use of speech or eyesight of one or more individuals or their ability to use certain limbs (where safe to do so.)

Obstacles
Introduce pre-determined, or random obstacles which aim to impede or slow the progress of your group, such as water, bridges, and 'safe' and 'unsafe' contact areas.

Scenario
There are generally three broad scenario options to choose from:

- Present the activity as it is, eg get your group from here to there in 30 minutes;

- As a fantasy, eg you have to save the pink Zulu elephants from a tribe of rampaging pygmies; or

- As a metaphor to reflect a number of key 'real-world' elements to help the activity make more sense to your group.

Keep in mind, the first four variables can be used as form of penalty if you choose, perhaps wrapped in a particular scenario. For example, if you do not cross the proverbial peanut-butter pit within 30 minutes, the island you are standing on (represented by a circle of rope) will get smaller.

4. Notes On Safety

Finally, it is important to consider the safety aspects of each activity, and to address the concerns that each one presents. Remember, no-prop activities involve the same risk management concerns that activities using equipment do: be aware of your environment, hazards and terrain, group ability, readiness, clothing and so on.

When briefing the activities in this book, point out hazards in the play area that may cause harm, such as dips in terrain. If the grass is wet and slippery, be especially wary of doing running games. Issues of terrain and environment are one of the primary reasons that group games produce more injuries than more dramatic high-adventure activities.

Additionally, be aware of medical and physical issues in your group that may cause a particular activity to be inappropriate. Shoulder injuries, sprained ankles and back problems are common, and can be exacerbated given the nature of some activities.

All of the essential programmatic tools described in this book are more than just a useful framework to help you lead powerful and rewarding programs. They are also important tools in keeping people safe – physically, emotionally and mentally. Make sure you group understands that they have choices, and then honour them.

Finally, be on the look-out for group readiness. Do participants have the skills to perform the activity? Has a particular person been seen to be somewhat unsteady on their feet? Lack of readiness can also put a group at risk.

To help you make well-informed decisions, follow the sequential framework of *The Difference Model* (Chapter 4) and the GRABBSS model (Chapter 15) to increase the chances of a safe and positive experience for all.

CHAPTER 7

Group-Splitting Ideas

One of the first things we often want to do when faced with a large group is to split them into smaller groupings, teams or pairs.

This chapter describes dozens of inventive, simple and fun ways to split large groups into smaller groups (including pairs) beyond the tired and boring routine of 'Okay, pick a partner' or the old count-off method of '1, 2, 3, 4, 1, 2, 3, 4...'

Activities that split large groups into smaller groups and partners feature:

- Creative, random and non-traditional splitting methods
- Very simple instructions
- Generally rapid execution
- Communication and critical-thinking skills

Generally speaking, the splitting process is devoted to achieving one of two objectives – to create groups of two people (pairs) or smaller teams of three or more people.

Some of my favourite group-splitting ideas are described here:

Getting Into Pairs – Getting Into Teams – Vowel Orchestra – Empowered Teams

Also, take a look at **Categories**, **Psychic Handshake** and **Clumps** which are categorised as Icebreakers in this book and happen to be equally useful as random group-splitting strategies.

Getting Into Pairs

Fun partner-matching strategies based on random criteria.

Benefits

- Simple, rapid pairing
- Very playful & fun
- Promotes interaction
- Non-traditional
- Breaks down cliques

People 4+

Time   1-2 mins

Instructions

1. Assemble your group.

1. Ask everyone to find one other person who also identifies with a particular criteria you announce.

2. For example, ask each person to find someone else who has the same or similar:
    - Colour top, pants, socks, etc.
    - Type of shoes worn.
    - Month or season of birth.
    - Length of hair.
    - Height, or size of hands, feet, thumb, ears, etc.
    - Colour of eyes or hair.
    - Favourite car, animal, ice-cream flavour, TV show, etc.
    - Same last digit of their street address.
    - Same last digit of their telephone number.
    - Choice of three holiday destination possibilities, eg Hawaii, Swiss alps, Hong Kong.
    - Favourite genre of movie, sport, book, etc.
    - Number of letters, syllables or vowels in their name.

Variations

- See **Look Up Look Down.** When two people happen to look at each other (ie by chance) they depart the scene as newly-formed partners, the circle contracts, and the pairing continues.

- See **Mute Line-Up.** Once the line is formed, fold the line in the middle so that each person ends up facing another person to become partners.

Getting Into Teams

Fun team-forming strategies based on random criteria.

Benefits

- Simple, rapid technique
- Very playful & fun
- Promotes interaction
- Non-traditional
- Breaks down cliques

People 4+

Time 1-2 mins

Instructions

1. Assemble your group.

2. Ask everyone to find all other people who also identify with a particular criteria you announce.

3. For simple **two-group splits**, ask each person to find all others who:
   - Prefer tea over coffee.
   - Arm that ends up crossed over the top of the other, when folded on your chest.
   - Shower or bath in the morning or end of the day.
   - Preference for cooking or cleaning up.
   - Born in first-half or second-half of the year.
   - Prefer a dog or a cat as a pet.
   - Position of your thumbs, that is left or right on top, when you clasp your hands together so that your fingers interlock.
   - Last digit of your home telephone number – odds or evens.
   - Number of street you live at – odds or evens.
   - Preference for bad news followed by good news, or vice-versa.

4. For simple **multi-group splits**, ask each person to find all others who:
   - Born in the same month (12 groups.)
   - Born in the same season of the year (4 groups.)
   - Number of siblings in your family, including yourself (1, 2, 3, 4 ...)
   - Oldest, youngest, or in-between in your family (3 groups.)
   - Which shoulder(s) you hold a carry-bag – right, left or both shoulders (3 groups.)
   - Mode of transport to get to the program (car, bus, bike, walk.)

Variations

- In pairs, ask one person to kneel down next to their partner. Invite all those who are standing to form one team, and all those who are kneeling to form the other team. A great way to separate friends or cliques.
- Start with **Getting Into Pairs**, ask each partnership to join with another pair. These four people join with another four people, etc, until you have the required number of teams.

Vowel Orchestra

Unique musical method to create random teams.

Benefits

- Very playful & fun
- Promotes interaction
- Non-traditional
- Breaks down cliques

People 8+

Time 1-2 mins

Instructions

1. Assemble your group.
2. Ask everyone to think of the first vowel of their first name.
3. On "GO" everyone makes the sound of this vowel loudly and constantly as they mingle with others.
4. Mingling continues until every person who is singing the same sound finds each other.
5. A maximum of five different groups may form.

Variations

- Use the first vowel of a person's last name.
- Ask people to sing the sound of the initial (first letter) of their first name. This technique will attract sounds of a similar harmony, eg everyone whose name starts with an E, D, P or T will associate with the EEEs.

Empowered Teams

Dynamic team-forming strategy controlled by your group.

Benefits

- Empowers your group
- Simple to set-up
- Critical-thinking
- Communication

People 10+

Time 2-5 mins

Instructions

1. Assemble your group.

2. Announce that you want your group to form into a specified number of teams.

3. Explain that each team must have the same number of members, and achieve a balance of the following criteria:
   - Gender
   - Age
   - Experience and/or Qualifications
   - Culture and/or Ethnicity
   - Other as useful to your purposes

4. Allow several minutes for your group to achieve task.

Variation

- Ask your group to split according to their own needs and wishes, into as many groups as you command. This strategy is very empowering, but the exercise may result in largely uneven teams.

CHAPTER 8

Ice-Breakers & Get-To-Know-You Games

Ice-breakers set the tone, invite people to play, interact and most importantly, laugh. In my opinion, breaking the 'ice' is the most critical (and often least-prepared) part of a program.

These activities provide an opportunity for the members of your group to 'get-to-know-each-other' and begin to feel more comfortable within the group. Even if the people know each other well, ice-breakers will always start your program with a few laughs.

Ice-breakers and get-to-know-you games typically feature:

- Fun as a major component
- Lots of non-threatening interaction
- Easy to understand instructions
- Success-oriented experiences
- Minimal verbal and decision-making skills
- 1 to 20 minutes of play

Large Group Interaction

Categories – Clumps – Spectrums – Crosstown Connections – Five Handshakes In Five Minutes – Ice-Breaker Question Exchange – Vortex – Making Connections – Let Me Introduce – Psychic Handshake – Elevator Air – Train Station Greetings – Identity Crisis

Partner Interaction

Paired Shares – Tiny Teach

Also, take a look at **Must Choose** and **This Or That** which are categorised as Trust-Building Exercises in this book and are equally useful as strategies to help your group get to know one another.

Categories

Highly-interactive exercise to create smaller groupings.

Benefits

- Simple, rapid execution
- Highly-interactive
- Breaks down cliques
- Fun method to form random groups

People 10+

Time 1-5 mins

Instructions

1. Assemble your group.
2. Announce a particular category, such as 'colour of eyes.'
3. Ask everyone to find all other people in the group who identify with the same category.
4. Repeat, with a series of two-group and multi-group categories, to mix your group.

Variations

- There are no shortage of category types you could announce, for example:
  - Preference for good or bad news first when both are presented to you
  - Favourite movie genre/hot beverage
  - Number of televisions in your home
  - Number of materials recycled at home
  - Type of shoes you are wearing (not necessarily their brand)
  - Preference for the way toilet paper spills off the roll – forwards, like a waterfall, or backwards against the wall
  - Leg you put into your pants, shorts, underwear, etc first when dressing
  - Side of the bed you (typically) get out of in the morning (as you are lying in it, facing the ceiling).

Reflection

- What did you notice as the activity progressed? What did you hear and see?
- What outcomes were achieved during this exercise?
- What might this exercise say about our individuality?

Clumps

One of the best rapid-fire group-mixing exercises ever.

Benefits

- Extremely quick
- Highly-interactive
- Raises energy
- Encourages sharing

People 8+

Time 5-10 mins

Instructions

1. Assemble your group.
2. Explain that everyone will soon be invited to form a series of smaller groups.
3. Each group will comprise a defined number of people matching the number you announce. For example, if you announce "SIX," everyone must form small groups of six people, including themselves.
4. Loudly announce the first number.
5. Encourage people to locate or form their groups quickly.
6. Upon gathering, consider asking the group to complete a task.
7. Repeat, by continuing to announce a series of numbers.

Variations

- When a new number is called, an individual cannot form a group with anyone who was in their previous group (as much as is possible – the larger the group, the easier this is to achieve.)
- Combine with **Paired-Shares** to invite sharing among members of each newly-formed small group.

Reflection

- What did you notice as the activity progressed?
- What outcomes were achieved during this exercise?
- What did it feel like when you could not form part of a group? How did you respond?

Spectrums

*Simple, non-verbal strategy to get
to know others quickly.*

Benefits

- Non-threatening
- Highly-interactive
- Promotes critical-thinking
- Great conversation starter

People 8+

Time 10-15 mins

black . . . . white

Instructions

1. Establish an imaginary line which extends between two ends of a spectrum, eg no energy to high energy.
2. Pose questions or scenarios inviting each person to consider their preferred response.
3. Invite everyone to stand at a point along the line, between the two ends of the spectrum, which most-closely reflects their preference.
4. Once positioned, ask each person to note the spread or otherwise of the group and their position within it.
5. For added value, invite individuals to share with people close to them.
6. Repeat process several times.

Variations

- There are no shortage of questions or scenarios you could ask, for example:
    - Exercise regime – never or several hours a day
    - Job preference – totally indoors or totally outdoors
    - Preferred group role – leader or follower
    - Preferred pet – cat or dog
    - Preferred taste – savoury or sweet
- Use this technique to process or debrief your group's experience, eg you could create a spectrum from Poor to Excellent to define how effective your group worked together.

Reflection

- Did anything surprise you about this exercise?
- Were you surprised by the positions of others, or yourself relative to others?
- What might any one of these results say about our group?

Crosstown Connections

Rapid & highly-interactive greeting exercise for groups.

Benefits

- Very playful & fun
- Highly-interactive
- Inspires creativity
- Ideal for forming random partners

People 8+

Time 10-15 mins

Instructions

1. Demonstrate a particular handshake with a volunteer, eg high-five.

2. Invite everyone to find one partner, according to random criteria you nominate, to practice this greeting.

3. Demonstrate a second handshake or greeting with a new volunteer, eg fist-bump.

4. Again, invite everyone to find a new partner – according to new nominated criteria – to practice this latest handshake.

5. Introduce two or three more unique handshake or greetings, asking people to find a new partner each time.

6. For fun and to reinforce established partnerships, randomly call the name of a particular greeting to challenge everyone to quickly locate their relevant partner.

Variations

- Take a minute or two between greetings to ask each person to share their response to a question you pose. See **Ice-Breaker Questions Exchange** for plenty of options.

- Challenge your group to greet every one of their partners in the order they were introduced as quickly as possible.

Reflection

- Which greetings did you enjoy the most? Why?
- What techniques did you use to remember your various partners?
- Why are greetings – of any type – important?

Five Handshakes In Five Minutes

Energetic mixing & greeting exercise for new groups.

Benefits

- Simple, yet playful
- Highly-interactive
- Generates lots of energy
- Inspires creativity

People 8+

Time 2-5 mins

Instructions

1. Assemble your group.

2. Introduce a series of fun handshake greetings, one at a time.

3. For example, and by demonstration with a volunteer, engage in a typical 'high-five' greeting.

4. Invite each person to engage in a 'high-five' greeting with as many people in the group as possible in less than 20 seconds.

5. Demonstrate a second innovative handshake greeting, eg a fist-bump, inviting your group to try it with as many people as possible in less than 20 seconds.

6. Repeat this process with three more interesting greetings.

Variations

- Invite each pair to introduce themselves before getting stuck into a greeting.

- In pairs, ask your group to develop one or more zany handshakes, and then invite a number of volunteer pairs to demonstrate their creations.

Reflection

- How did you feel when the exercise was first introduced? Did that feeling change?

- Are you inspired to share a unique handshake or greeting you know with the group?

- When was the last time you experienced something which invited you to step outside your Comfort Zone?

Ice-Breaker Question Exchange

Simple get-to-know-you game that encourages sharing.

Benefits

- Very simple
- Non-threatening
- Highly-interactive
- Encourages sharing

People 8+

Time 15-20 mins

Instructions

1. In advance, prepare a large list of non-threatening 'ice-breaker' type questions. Or, scan the QR code below to access dozens of sample questions as a subscriber.

2. Form into pairs.

3. Pose your first question to the group.

4. Invite each person to ask their partner for a response, and vice-versa.

5. After each person has shared, swap partners and/or pose your second question.

6. Continue process of sharing and/or partner-swapping for 10 to 20 minutes.

Variations

- Form groups of three or more people, inviting each person in the group to respond to each question, before disbanding and then seeking new partners to form a new group.

- Replace the questions with actions, eg 'Perform ten star-jumps in a row,' 'Shake the hand of five different people within 30 seconds,' and 'Run around the outside of the group as quickly as possible.'

Reflection

- What did you notice as the activity progressed?

- How would you describe the atmosphere within which you shared? Did this assist or limit your sharing?

- In the context of our group, is this type of sharing important or beneficial?

Vortex

Guided & interactive series of partner conversations.

Benefits

- Simple to set-up
- Highly-interactive
- Encourages conversation
- Structured

People 12+

Time 15-20 mins

Instructions

1. Form into pairs.

2. One person in each pair is assigned number 1, the other is number 2.

3. Invite all number 1 people to form a large circle facing outwards, and ask all number 2 people to stand directly in front of and face their partners.

4. Pose a question which invites each pair to have a short conversation.

5. After a minute or two, ask one of the circles (numbers 1 or 2) to rotate to the left (or right) a specified number of places, so that everyone faces a new partner, eg outside circle, move three people to your right.

6. Continue this process of changing partners several times, asking a different question each time.

Variations

- Ask everyone who is wearing a particular coloured garment, say red, to swap spots with their partners. This will mix some of the '1's with the '2's providing a chance for some '1's to meet a '1' and vice versa.

- Introduce a series of fun and active partner-only exercises for each new partnership, eg **Thumb-Wrestling In Stereo**, **Gotcha** and **One-Two-Three**.

Reflection

- Name two or three new things you learned about other people today?
- What did the group learn about you, that until now, was not widely known?
- How does this activity make you feel towards the group? Why?

Making Connections

Simple ice-breaker to connect group members to others.

Benefits

- Simple to understand
- Terrific get-to-know-you game
- Inspires critical-thinking
- Circle game

People 8

Time 2-5 mins

Instructions

1. Gather your group in a large open space.
2. Ultimate objective is to create one large circle in which every person is physically linked with two others.
3. Ask one volunteer to stand with one hand on their hip, and then share one or more statements about themselves to the group.
4. When someone from the rest of the group hears a statement that they have in common with the first volunteer, they are invited to link elbows with them.
5. This second person then shares something about themselves to the larger group, to attract a new person to link elbows with them, and so on.
6. This process of sharing and linking continues one by one.
7. To complete the circle, invite the last person to join the long chain of connections to share something about themselves to link with the very first volunteer.

Variations

- In very large groups, start with several 'first' volunteers, and invite just as many smaller circles to be formed. Allow the groups to form organically, or instruct each group to only attract a specified number of people.
- One person shares one sentence to begin a (fictional) story, and with each new volunteer who links up, the story continues to build.

Reflection

- What new things did you learn about other members of your group?
- Were you nervous for it to be your turn? Why?
- How did creativity come into play in this activity? What's an example?

Let Me Introduce

Unique & highly-interactive method of introductions.

Benefits

- Simple
- Innovative
- Highly-interactive
- Generates energy

People 12+

Time 1-2 mins

> Harry, let me introduce Suzi to you...

Instructions

1. Assemble your group, standing together.
2. Start by approaching a random person and ask them to say their name.
3. Lead this person to another random person in the group, and ask this person to say their name.
4. Using each of their names, introduce the first person to the second person, eg "Simon this is Vijay, Vijay meet Simon."
5. All three of you now seek a new person to meet, or submit to another person's invitation to be a part of their introduction.
6. Allow several minutes of mingling and greeting one another.

Variations

- Invite one of the two people who have just been introduced to each other to lead the other to a new person. Continuing the example above, Simon could lead Vijay to meet and greet with Rachel.
- Announce that your group has two minutes to introduce everyone to everybody else. It won't happen, but that's not the point.

Reflection

- How did you feel when the exercise was first introduced? Did that feeling change?
- Did you ever feel the urge to introduce yourself? Why?
- What did you notice as the activity progressed?

Psychic Handshake

*Innovative, random & fun
group-splitting technique.*

Benefits

- Simple, rapid execution
- Highly-interactive
- Breaks down cliques
- Random group-splitting method

People 8+

Time 1-2 mins

Instructions

1. Assuming you need four groups, ask everyone to think of a number 1, 2, 3 or 4 (adapt as necessary.)

2. Invite each person to mingle and shake hands with as many people as possible.

3. Each person should only shake their own hand (and arm) the number of times of the number they are thinking, and then firmly stop shaking.

4. When two people shake hands the same number of times, they belong in the same group.

5. No talking, extending fingers or clapping is allowed, but laughter is permitted.

6. Invite people to continue interacting with others until every one discovers their group, and the required number of groups has been formed.

Variations

- Same set-up, use left arms only.
- Same set-up, blindfolded.

Reflection

- How clear was your communication (shaking) in the beginning?
- What did you do to ensure your message was clearly received? Why?
- How confident were you that you and others were in the correct group?

Elevator Air

Powerful exercise to set the tone & teach responsibility.

Benefits

- Simple
- Non-threatening
- Inspires critical-thinking
- Powerful metaphor

People 8+

Time 10-15 mins

Instructions

1. Form a large circle.
2. Ask each person to cross to the other side 'as if' they were in an elevator.'
3. Upon crossing, ask the group to describe the atmosphere this crossing created.
4. Ask each person to cross a second time, this time imagining they were in a car driving on the highway.
5. Upon crossing, ask the group to describe the atmosphere this second crossing created.
6. Ask each person to cross a final time, this time imagining they were at a party with their long-lost friends.
7. Upon crossing, ask the group to describe the atmosphere this third crossing created.
8. Process the experience, distinguishing the three outcomes each crossing created, and why they were different.

Variations

- As above, silently.
- Consider three distinct scenarios related to starting a new job, or school, in regards how people choose to interact – Awkward, Polite, Enthusiastic.

Reflection

- How was it possible that we achieved three different outcomes?
- What caused each crossing to be different? Who was in control?
- What is the impact of this understanding on you, the group, the program?

Train Station Greetings

Chaotic, interactive game that inspires slow-motion moves.

Benefits

- Very playful & fun
- Highly-interactive
- Inspires creativity
- Builds trust

People 15+

Time 1-2 mins

Instructions

1. Form pairs.
2. Spread your group throughout a wide, open area, requesting that partners position themselves a long distance away from one another.
3. By demonstration with a volunteer, act out a slow-motion scene involving the two of you greeting each other from a distance.
4. You approach one another slowly until approximately 2 metres (7') apart.
5. Then suddenly, you realise that you have mistaken the identity of this person.
6. Swiftly, you look away and spy another person to repeat the whole greeting-from-afar process again.
7. Continue play for 1 to 2 minutes.

Variations

- As above, completely silent, as if it was a silent movie.
- Alter the states in which people greet each other – fast-motion, sleepy-motion, drunken-motion, short-sighted (regular speed,) etc.

Reflection

- Did you feel silly playing this game? Why?
- Is it okay to behave in a silly manner sometimes?
- What sort of atmosphere do you or a group need to behave this way?

Identity Crisis

Hilarious get-to-know-you-more game for large groups.

Benefits

- Inventive name-game
- Ideal for new & familiar groups
- Sharpens listening skills
- Highly-interactive

People 8+

Time 10-15 mins

Instructions

1. Pose three questions and invite everyone to consider their responses, eg favourite movie, ideal holiday location, and what they would do if they won the lottery.

2. Over the course of the next few minutes, invite everyone to have a short conversation with a series of partners introducing themselves, especially sharing these three bits of information.

3. After this mutual exchange, instruct partners to swap identities, ie each person assumes the identity of their partner, including the three bits of information they just learned about their partner.

4. Each person then seeks a new partner, introducing themselves with their new identity.

5. Continue playing for 10 or more minutes, inviting each person to complete as many exchanges (and swaps of identity) as possible.

6. To conclude, form a circle, and invite each person to introduce their current identity (including their three bits of information) to the group.

Variation

- Invite each person to share their information non-verbally or with charade-like manner.

Reflection

- What did it feel like to forget or tell the wrong information? Why?
- Why do we put so much pressure on ourselves to remember people's names?
- What strategies do you use to remember names and information about others?

Paired Shares

Non-threatening strategy to invite sharing in a group.

Benefits

- Very simple
- Non-threatening
- Promotes communication
- Partner activity

People 2+

Time 1-2 mins

Instructions

1. Form into small groups of two or three people.
2. Pose your question, and invite each person to share their response(s) with their partners.
3. Continue to ask questions, or swap partners.

Variations

- If you have a series of questions, invite your group to mix, so that each person has the opportunity to share with many others, but still within the relative safety of a pair.
- Form two circles comprising an even number of people, one inside the other. Pair people in one circle to the other circle. After one or more questions, ask one circle to rotate a specified number of people to the left (or right) to initiate a conversation with a new partner. Take a look at **Vortex** for more details.

Reflection

- How did it feel to share with your partner or small group? Why?
- Did you learn something you did not know a few minutes ago?
- Describe the type of environment you think is conducive to sharing openly with others?

Tiny Teach

Creative partner exercise to practice playful skills.

Benefits

- Very playful & fun
- Inspires creativity
- Fosters collaboration
- Partner activity

People 2+

Time 10-15 mins

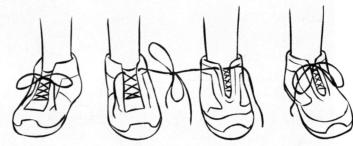

Instructions

1. Form into pairs.
2. Explain that you will shortly announce a series of quick partner activities.
3. Demonstrate the first partner activity, and then ask each pair to try it, eg whistle with your lips.
4. Continue to introduce more partner activities for each pair to try, tell a joke, whistle into your hands, tie a pair of shoe-laces, etc.
5. Swap partners, and/or invite each person to teach a skill they know to their partner.

Variations

- In pairs, each partner demonstrates and teaches the method they use to tie their shoe-laces.
- In pairs or small groups, share a short but fun activity or game they enjoy with the rest of the group.

Reflection

- Could you think of a skill to share with your partner quickly? Why or why not?
- What helped you successfully impart your knowledge to another person? What didn't help?
- Describe your experience of passing on a newly-learned skill to others?

CHAPTER 9

Name-Games

Here are a bunch of fun get-to-know-you games that specifically encourage and enable people to learn one another's names. There is no doubt that the higher the level of name-knowingness, the more fun (and trust) your group will develop.

The name-games I describe here feature:

- Fun and laughter as vital ingredients
- Lots of non-threatening interaction
- Emphasis on effort, rather than results
- Ample opportunities to hear and learn names
- Small and large group interactions
- 1 to 15 minutes of play

Small Group Interaction

Story Of Your Name – That Ain't Me Babe – Kram Dralloc

Whole Group Interaction

Who? – What's In A Name – Imaginary Toss-A-Name Game – Me You You Me
Fill Me In – Zombie Name-Game – Name Roulette – Cocktail Party
Bumpity Bump Bump Bump – Name Impulse – Turbo Name-Game

Story of Your Name

Fascinating name-game to break the ice & build trust.

Benefits

- Simple
- Powerful name-game
- Endlessly fascinating
- Ideal for partners

People 2+

Time 2-5 mins

Instructions

1. Divide into small groups of two, three or four people.

2. Instruct each person to take turns and share the story of their full name with their partner(s.)

3. By way of demonstration, share the origin of your first, middle and last names with your group.

4. Allow ample time for sharing to occur.

5. Optional – once all small groups have shared, invite one or more volunteers to share anything interesting that they learned about their partners to the large group.

Variations

- Invite people to focus on sharing the story of just one part of your name (their choice.) Middle names are often good value topics, because parents often like to acknowledge significant names there.

- Share the story of why a certain 'object' (eg pet, favourite piece of clothing, your car, etc) is named.

Reflection

- How did it feel to share a little of the history of your name?
- Were you fascinated by the origins of your partner's names? Why?
- Do you think everyone has something special to share about their name?

That Ain't Me Babe

*Fun & creative action-oriented
name-game for small groups.*

Benefits

- Very playful & fun
- Promotes creativity
- Sharpens observation skills
- Action-oriented

People 8+

Time 5-10 mins

Instructions

1. Form into pairs, or small groups of three or four (at most.)

2. Taking turns, explain that each person will be invited to mime three 'things' about themselves to their partner, eg what they do for a living, where they live, a hobby.

3. Explain that no one is permitted to talk, ask questions or perform any part of their mime a second time.

4. Once each person has mimed their story, gather your group together again.

5. Invite one person at a time to introduce their partner to the rest of the group, highlighting, in particular, a description of what they observed.

6. Continue until everyone has introduced their partner.

Variations

- Ask each person to mime an interesting or funny scene from their life, for the purposes of having it re-told by their partner.

- More challenging – invite the observing partner to mime what they saw back to the group, and ask the group to guess what it is they are communicating (about their partner.)

Reflection

- Was it difficult to not talk (verbally) as you were telling your story? What was hard?

- What signals from your partner did you observe that indicated that they understood what you said, or otherwise?

- How might you improve your ability to communicate next time?

Kram Dralloc

Zany name-game to break the ice & generate laughter.

Benefits

- Hilarious
- Extremely fun & playful
- Inspires creativity
- Ideal for familiar groups

People 2+

Time 2-5 mins

Instructions

1. Gather your group as one large group, or divide into smaller groups for greater intimacy.

2. One by one, ask each person to say their name out loud to the others as if the letters of their name were arranged in reverse.

3. Demonstrate by sharing your own name first, eg Mark Collard becomes Kram Dralloc.

4. Next, ask the group to speculate where in the world would a person with that name live if it were real.

5. Continue around the group until everyone has shared.

Variations

- Combine the first letter of your first name with the first two letters of your surname to create a little hyphenated moniker.

- In small groups, ask each person to invent a nonsensical acronym of their first (or second) name, and then present it to the larger group. For example, KEVIN becomes Kangaroos Eat Vegetables In November and MARK could represent Magic Ankle Repair Kit.

Reflection

- How difficult was it for you to think of your name backwards? Why?
- This exercise often triggers spontaneous bursts of laughter. Why?
- For a good laugh, what other areas of our lives could we apply this silly game to?

Who?

Fun name-game for large groups who don't know each other.

Benefits

- Simple
- Ideal for large groups
- Highly-interactive
- Fosters communication

People 8+

Time 5-10 mins

Instructions

1. Form a large circle, with you in the centre.
2. Start by pointing randomly at one person standing as part of the circle and calling "WHO?" out loud.
3. As you move towards this pointed-to person, they will respond by calling out their name loudly, and immediately step in towards the centre of the circle.
4. Swap roles with the pointed-to person, as you move into the newly-departed place of this person in the circle.
5. The game continues with this new person in the centre pointing and calling "WHO?" to another person standing in the circle, causing these two people to swap roles, and so on.
6. After several minutes of play, introduce two, three or more people into the centre to involve more people.

Variations

- As the pointer and pointed-to people move past one another (trading places,) ask them to shake hands and/or engage in a brief greeting of sorts.
- Ask the person doing the pointing to repeat the name they just heard (from the person they pointed to) as they exchange a greeting in passing.

Reflection

- Do you often find it difficult to remember names?
- When you forget the name of a person you have met before, what strategies do you use to avoid looking bad when interacting with them again?
- What systems or techniques do you use to help you remember names?

What's In A Name

Innovative series of games involving people's full names.

Benefits

- Very simple
- Reinforces names
- Celebrates diversity
- Inspires critical-thinking

People 8+

Time 5-10 mins

Instructions

1. Ask everyone to tally the number of letters in their first name.

2. Instruct your group to form one straight line from lowest to the highest number of letters.

3. Individuals may choose to adopt an abbreviated version of their name, provided they are ordinarily known by that name.

4. Award nominal gold medals to those whose names comprise the lowest and highest number of letters.

5. Next, add the number of letters comprising their first and middle names, and re-arrange themselves from highest to lowest number of letters accordingly.

6. Finally, calculate the total number of letters in their full names – first, middle and last names – and re-arrange themselves from highest to lowest number of letters.

7. Offer celebratory applause for each round of gold medal performance.

Variations

- Allow only single instances of each letter of the alphabet, ie if a letter appears more than once in a person's name(s,) it can only be counted once. For example, Alexander comprises only seven letters, because he can only count the letters A and E once.

- Work your way through the entire alphabet (A to Z) and score a point every time a particular letter is not represented (at least once) in the full names of their entire group. Aim to score zero points.

Reflection

- What is it like to have a long or difficult to pronounce name?
- How did it feel to have your name valued in this exercise?
- What could this game teach us about valuing diversity in our groups?

Imaginary Toss-A-Name Game

Creative name-game that inspires fun & imagination.

Benefits

- Simple
- Highly-interactive
- Inspires creativity
- Ideal for new groups

People 8+

Time 10-15 mins

Instructions

1. Standing in a circle, ask everyone to say their name one at a time clockwise around the circle.

2. Upon returning to you, repeat this process in the other direction.

3. Ask a volunteer to call the name of another person in the circle to attract their attention, and then pass an imaginary object to them, eg basketball.

4. Each person who receives this object repeats this process, eg call name, get attention, pass object.

5. After several minutes, introduce more 'objects' to involve more people, as appropriate.

6. Introduce one or more variations to vary the pace and type of passing.

7. Finally, stop the passing, and ask one or more volunteers to recall as many names as they can.

Variations

- Ask the people who receive an 'object' to say "THANK YOU" to the person who tossed it to them, but importantly, using that person's name.

- The tosser will attract the attention of the person to whom they wish to pass, but does not call his or her name. Instead, as the person receives the pass, everyone in the circle calls out the receiver's name. Great for people who have trouble remembering names.

Reflection

- Did this exercise help you remember more names more quickly? Why?
- What strategies do you use to help you remember names?
- What moment in this exercise sticks out in your mind? Why?

Me You You Me

Hilarious, interactive name-game for small groups.

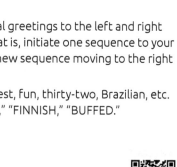

Benefits

- Introductory name-game
- Triggers spontaneous laughter
- Encourages interaction
- Ideal for small groups

People 8+

Time 5-10 mins

Instructions

1. Form a circle, including yourself.
2. Step inside the circle, and face your left-hand side neighbour.
3. Shaking hands, say your own name, and your neighbour says their name.
4. You repeat your neighbour's name, and they say your name, then stop shaking.
5. Move to your right, and repeat the process with the next person in the circle.
6. When you reach the third person in the circle, the first person you greeted steps inside the circle and initiates a greeting with their left-hand side neighbour.
7. Process continues, until everyone has greeted all others in the circle at least once.
8. Ultimately, everyone returns to their original spot in the circle.

Variations

- Got a large group of say 30 or 50 people? Start the initial greetings to the left and right direction of the break in the circle at the same time. That is, initiate one sequence to your left as normal, and then after a few exchanges, start a new sequence moving to the right (or the circle) from whence you were standing.
- Describe something interesting about yourself, eg honest, fun, thirty-two, Brazilian, etc. For example, it may sound like this "BUFFED," "FINNISH," "FINNISH," "BUFFED."

Reflection

- At what point did this exercise trigger laughter? Why?
- What was the most challenging part of the game?
- What was the most enjoyable part of the game?

Fill Me In

Active circle name-game with lots of fun variations.

Benefits

- Simple
- Highly-interactive
- Non-threatening
- Active

People 8+

Time 5-10 mins

Instructions

1. Form a large circle, with ample space between people.
2. One person steps into the circle, pointing to and calling the name of another person.
3. This named-person will then immediately swap positions with the person who called their name.
4. Now, in the centre of the circle, this recently named-person calls the name of another person.
5. This process of naming and swapping positions repeats itself over and over.
6. After a minute or two, introduce two or more people who can point and announce the name of others in the circle.

Variations

- Invite everyone to move briskly, or to hop, jump, walk sideways, etc.
- Invite the person who has called out a name, to introduce themselves by name to the other, perhaps shake hands as they trade places, before this newly-named person repeats the process.

Reflection

- Did you ever stumble to know what to do the moment someone called your name? Why?
- In general, did you choose people you knew or did not know so well? Why?
- What helped you to remember a few new names?

Zombie Name-Game

Quirky circle name-game with lots of fun movements.

Benefits

- Playful & fun
- Inspires creativity
- Great energiser
- Active

People 8+

Time 5-10 mins

Instructions

1. Form a circle, including yourself.
2. Loudly call the name of a person standing in the circle and start walking towards them, acting like a 'zombie' with your arms stretched out in front of you.
3. Your aim is to tag this named-person on their shoulders.
4. This named-person aims to call the name of another person in the circle before they are tagged.
5. If they avoid being tagged, the original named-person will immediately step into the circle and attempt to tag the person they just named.
6. On all occasions, the openings in the circle are filled by the previous zombie.
7. If the named-person is tagged, everyone can enjoy a good laugh and, after a few moments, invite the tagged-person to become the next zombie.
8. Play for several minutes, introducing extra 'zombies' as appropriate.

Variations

- Introduce a second, third and fourth zombie into the action, to occupy more people and generate more energy
- Eliminate anyone who is tagged by a zombie. With each elimination, the circle contracts until only three people remain – declare them all winners.

Reflection

- What did it feel like to walk like a 'zombie.'
- How did you feel to watch a 'zombie' walk towards you? Why?
- As a zombie, did you choose people you knew or did not know so well? Why?

Name Roulette

Fun, movement-based name-game ideal for familiar groups.

Benefits

- Playful & fun
- Ideal for all groups
- Highly-interactive
- Many variations

People 16+

Time 10-15 mins

Instructions

1. Divide your group into two relatively even teams.
2. Each team forms a circle by holding hands facing into the circle.
3. Position the circles so that the outside edge of each circle passes over a designated spot, eg hula-hoop lying on ground.
4. Each team rotates their circle, in any direction, always passing a part of their circle over the designated spot.
5. Randomly and simultaneously tap the shoulders of one person from each team when they are passing over the designated spot.
6. Upon being tapped, the two circles stop moving as these two people spin around and attempt to name the other as quickly as possible to earn a point for their team.
7. Play continues for several minutes.
8. The team with the most points wins.

Variations

- Turn music on and off to indicate when the circles have to stop, to identify which two people are the closest to the spot.
- Reward the 'winning' team by absorbing the firstly-named person into their circle, ie your circle gets bigger with every win.

Reflection

- What did you notice when people had to suddenly recall someone's name?
- Was it challenging to perform several tasks at the same time?
- Where else in our lives do we attempt to perform multiple tasks at the same time? Is this a good thing?

Cocktail Party

*Ice-breaker that invites people
to playfully mix & mingle.*

Benefits

- Simple
- Reinforces new names
- Highly-interactive
- Promotes communication

People 8+

Time 1-2 mins

Instructions

1. Gather your group rather closely around you, as if standing in a small room.

2. Ask everyone to hold out their left hand as if they were holding their favourite drink.

3. On "GO" everyone shakes hands and greets as many people in the room as possible.

4. Encourage people to use the name of the person they are greeting in the conversation.

5. For fun, announce your group has 43.5 seconds (or other nominal time) to achieve this task.

Variations

- For young people, or groups that may not imbibe alcohol, suggest they are holding their favourite (soft) drink.

- Imagine you are in a swanky food hall. Invite people to mingle as they treat themselves to the extraordinary array of fine foods available on people's food trays.

Reflection

- What did you notice as you mingled with others in the group?

- How many of you could remember the drinks other people were holding? Why do you think this occurred?

- How does the atmosphere of this artificial 'cocktail party' differ from the manner in which your group normally interacts?

Bumpity Bump Bump Bump

Quick circle name-game for groups that know each other.

Benefits

- Very playful & fun
- Name-reminder game
- Highly-interactive
- Sharpens reflexes

People 8+

Time 5-10 mins

Instructions

1. Form a circle, with you standing in the centre.

2. Point to a random person in the circle, saying one of four words – "LEFT," "RIGHT," "YOU" or "ME."

3. Each is an instruction for the person being pointed at to accurately name the person to their left or right, their own name or yours (person in the middle.)

4. The name must be uttered quicker than you (middle person) can say the words "BUMPITY BUMP BUMP BUMP."

5. If the correct name is called quickly enough, this person survives another round.

6. If they are too slow, or make a mistake, they are invited to swap roles with the person in the middle.

7. Play a couple of 'test' rounds to help your group practice.

8. After a few minutes, introduce one or more new people into the middle of the circle.

Variations

- For younger groups, or those with lesser name-retention abilities, limit the pointer to asking for the names of "LEFT" and "RIGHT" neighbours.

- Introduce the activity as an elimination, whereby the person in the centre remains there all the time, and continues pointing until the final two people are left standing.

Reflection

- Under pressure, how easy was it to recall the correct name? Why?

- What strategies did you employ to be successful?

- Where else in your life or work does pressure make an impact?

Name Impulse

Exciting get-to-know-you name-game for large groups.

Benefits

- Simple
- Great name-reminder
- Healthy competition
- Promotes communication

People 8+

Time 2-5 mins

Instructions

1. Form a circle, seated or standing.

2. Starting with the person to your left, ask them to say their name as soon as you give them a signal.

3. As soon as this person says their name, the person to their left calls our their name, and so on.

4. This impulse of names continues around the circle until it returns to where it started.

5. Next, record the time it takes the impulse of names to be called all around the circle.

6. Invite your group to make several attempts, and then change directions.

7. Note the best time.

Variations

- Send the impulse in both directions (A and B Teams) at the same time. Note which team was the fastest.

- Send something other than your name around the circle, eg a personal quality, value or favourite colour.

Reflection

- Did you notice the influence of pressure in your ability to perform (say your name?) What does this mean?

- Who was on the winning team?

- Did the group always adhere to the parameters of the exercise? Does this matter?

Turbo Name-Game

*Fast-paced, challenging name-reminder
& recall game.*

Benefits

- Quick to set-up
- Highly-interactive
- Challenging
- Ideal for familiar groups

People 8+

Time 5-10 mins

Instructions

1. Gather your group in an open, flat area.

2. Ask them to close their eyes and mingle randomly in the area until you say "STOP."

3. With eyes now open, everyone must remain standing in the same position until they are tagged on the shoulder.

4. To start, tap one person at random who must then quickly attempt to name and tag (in that order) another person in the group.

5. This process of naming and tagging is repeated until everyone has been tagged.

6. Encourage people who are tagged to step back out of the group to ensure they don't get tagged again.

7. Play several rounds to record the quickest time.

Variations

- As above, but everyone keeps their eyes closed until they are tagged.
- Ask the just-been-named to open their eyes and quickly call the name of any person they can identify to keep the ball rolling, ie no tagging.

Reflection

- What did you notice or feel as soon as your shoulder was tapped? Why?
- Did the pressure of a timed-event impact on your performance (recall of a name?)
- Where else in your life or work does pressure or stress impact on your performance?

CHAPTER 10

Energisers, Warm-Ups & Stretches

The activities featured in this chapter energise and warm people up, sometimes inviting them to stretch a little – physically, emotionally and mentally. They are perfect 'brain-boosters' as much as they provide opportunities for your group to interact, stretch and let off a little steam.

To be effective, energisers, warm-ups and stretches should feature:

- Fun as a major component
- Variety of physical and emotional challenges
- Opportunities to stimulate energy and attention
- Opportunities to interact
- Focus on effort and trying rather than success or failure
- 1 to 20 minutes of play

Partners

1-2-3-4 – One-Two-Three – Your Add – Mirror Stretch – Space Counting
Isometric Stretch – Thumb Wrestling In Stereo – Wiggle Waggle – Toe To Toe
Skipping Rope – Woodcutter's Warm-Up – Star Stretch – Windmill Stretch

Whole Group

Gotcha – People To People – Freeze Frame – Fill The Space
Mission Impossible – Count Off – Ro Sham Bo – ESP – Quick Line-Up
Shipwreck – Salt & Pepper – Around The World – I've Got The Power
Wave Stretch – Yurt Circle – Knee Impulse – Chic-A-Boom

1-2-3-4

Quick, small group energiser with lots of variations.

Nine!

Benefits

- Fast-paced
- Partner activity
- Stimulates energy
- Focus on mathematics

People 2+

Time 2-5 mins

Instructions

1. Form into small groups of two (or three) people, facing one another.

2. Instruct each person to shake one of their fists up and down at the same time as they chant "ONE, TWO, THREE, FOUR" together.

3. On "...FOUR," everyone extends any number of fingers from none to five on one hand.

4. Group aims to achieve exactly seven (or eleven) extended fingers.

5. No talking is permitted between the players at any time.

6. Challenge each group to achieve the sum of seven (or eleven) as often as possible within 60 seconds.

Variations

- Vary the number of people in a small group. For example, with three people, aim to produce 11 fingers.

- With each new round, an individual is required to extend a different number of fingers, ie to prevent the sneaky practice of knowing what to expect on each other's hands, thereby manipulating a result.

Reflection

- What did you think as soon as you realised that this game involved mathematics?

- How did your group respond when you achieved the desired sum? Did it take long?

- What else did you notice during the game?

One-Two-Three

Simple partner exercise to trigger bursts of laughter.

Benefits

- Very playful & fun
- Fosters critical-thinking
- Invites collaboration
- Partner activity

People 2+

Time 5-10 mins

Instructions

1. Form partners, with each person facing the other about 1 metre apart.
2. Each pair will aim to count out loud the numbers "1, 2, 3" with each person saying one number at a time, eg Jane says "1" and then Amber says "2," then Jane says "3," etc.
3. Pairs continue repeating this pattern of numbers as fast and accurately as possible.
4. After a short practice, explain that you want each pair to repeat the process but first substituting the calling of "1" with a clap over one's head, eg sounds like clap, two, three.
5. Then, after several rounds, repeat the process by substituting the calling of "2" with a little jump on the spot, eg sounds like clap, jump, three.
6. Finally, repeat the process by substituting the calling of "3" with the sound of a cat's meow, eg sounds like clap, jump meow.
7. Encourage each pair to complete the exercise as quickly, accurately and for as long as possible.
8. If a mistake is made, the pair should enjoy a good laugh and then start over.
9. Swap partners, or try a variation.

Variations

- Involve four people, standing in a circle facing each other.
- Vary the actions for each of the numbers. For example, perform a star-jump, bark like a dog, beat your chest, etc.

Reflection

- Was this exercise challenging? Why?
- What was your reaction when a mistake was made?
- Is it okay to make mistakes? Why, and in what circumstances?

Your Add

Quick & highly-interactive partner energiser.

Benefits

- Fast-paced
- Spontaneous fun
- Develops critical-thinking
- Partner activity

People 2+

Time 1-2 mins

Instructions

1. Form into pairs facing each other.
2. One partner begins by calling "SET" which will cause both partners to place their hands behind their backs and extend a certain number of fingers on one or both hands.
3. When ready, the other partner will call "GO" causing both people to thrust their hands forward so that all four hands can be seen.
4. The first person to call out the correct sum of all extended fingers, wins that round.
5. Play several rounds, then swap partners.

Variations

- Invite people to mix and mingle until they spy a willing partner to face-off with. This pair will engage in one or more rounds, and at some point, move on to find a new rival.
- Form teams of three or four people, and nominate one of them to be the 'multiplier' (their fingers are multiplied by the sum of all other fingers) or 'subtractor' (their fingers are subtracted from the sum of all other fingers.)

Reflection

- Was this quick exercise fun to play? Why or why not?
- What process did you adopt to add all of the fingers as quickly as possible?
- How did it feel to be the first one to correctly add the sum?

Mirror Stretch

Fun partner-stretching exercise with lots of twists.

Benefits

- Playful & fun
- Fosters collaboration
- Stimulates creativity
- Partner activity

People 2+

Time   2-5 mins

Instructions

1. Form pairs.
2. Each person stands and faces their partner about a metre apart (3'.)
3. One person initiates a series of zany, stretching movements.
4. The other person attempts to mimic the movements of their partner as if they were a 'mirror.'
5. Swap roles after 30 seconds, and then swap partners.

Variations

- Try the reverse-mirror stretch, during which the follower tries to mime exactly the opposite of their partner's movement. For example, when I move my left arm, you move your left arm.
- Repeat in groups of three or four people. One person performs the moves, while all others attempt to mimic them.

Reflection

- What part of this exercise was the most challenging? Why?
- Were there times when you struggled to mimic the exact mirror stretch of your partner? How did you respond?
- What do you think is the purpose of such activities?

Space Counting

Fun partner-mimicking exercise with powerful metaphors.

Benefits

- Generates energy
- Promotes collaboration
- Inspires powerful metaphors
- Multiple variations

People 2+

Time 5-10 mins

Instructions

1. Form pairs.
2. Each person faces their partner and extends their pointer finger in front of them, about 30cm (12") from the end of their partner's finger.
3. On "GO" each person attempts to draw (in the air) every number in sequence from 1 to 30 as quickly as possible.
4. The first person to reach 30 is entitled to pump their fist into the air to proclaim a win.
5. Swap partners and/or try a variation.

Variations

- The writing partner may choose to draw any ten numbers at random (between 1–30) but their partner's goal is the same – to trace as best as possible the identical path of their partner's finger.
- Use letters of the alphabet, both upper and lower case, instead of numbers.

Reflection

- What was the biggest challenge you encountered?
- What got in the way of achieving your goal?
- What might this exercise teach us about goal-setting, collaboration or problem-solving?

Isometric Stretch

Creative physical warm-up for partners of all abilities.

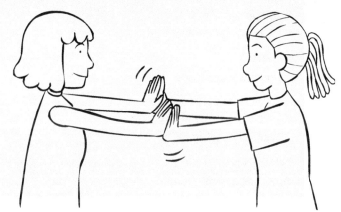

Benefits

- Inventive stretch
- Fosters collaboration
- Ideal PE warm-up
- Partner activity

People 2+

Time 2-5 mins

Instructions

1. Form pairs.

2. In an open space, ask each pair to explore as many different ways for two people to apply isometric pressure to their bodies.

3. For the purposes of this exercise, isometric is the equal application of pressure or resistance between two people who do not appear to be moving.

4. Provide a quick demonstration, such as two people facing each other and applying pressure to the open palms of their right hands in front of themselves.

5. Allow 2 to 3 minutes for each pair to discover multiple isometric positions.

6. If useful, swap partners.

Variations

- Invite one or more partners to demonstrate an inventive isometric stretch they enjoyed, and ask everyone to try it.
- Try groups of three or four people applying pressure isometrically to the same or variety of body parts.

Reflection

- Did it surprise you that it was possible to stretch and warm-up with little movement?
- How many different ways did you discover you could apply isometric pressure with your partner? How many were unique?
- How might the concept of 'isometric' apply elsewhere in our lives/work/play?

Thumb-Wrestling In Stereo

*Fun variation of the classic
thumb-wrestling contest.*

Benefits

- Friendly competition
- Highly-interactive
- Triggers spontaneous laughter
- Applies critical-thinking

People 2+

Time 1-2 mins

Instructions

1. Form partners.
2. Instruct each person to extend both their left and right hands and to curl their fingers inside the matching palms of their partner.
3. Starting with opposing thumbs side-by-side, each person aims to pin their partner's thumb under their own thumb first.
4. Best of five rounds wins.
5. Swap partners and repeat.

Variations

- Play with three or four people, all curling their fingers into one big clump of palm propinquity.
- Form a circle of thumb-wrestling holds, where every second person crosses their arms in front of themselves to grab their neighbour's matching hands. Once both thumbs of an individual have been pinned, they are eliminated and the circle re-joins. Continue until the Thumb-Wrestling Champion of the World is crowned.

Reflection

- What did you notice playing this classic game with two hands, rather than just one?
- What strategies did you employ to successfully pin your partner's thumb under your own?
- When your thumb was pinned, what was your immediate response? Why?

Wiggle Waggle

*Curious & dexterous physical stunt
to inspire play.*

Benefits

- Promotes play
- Develops critical-thinking
- Generates energy
- Partner activity

People 1+

Time 2-5 mins

Instructions

1. Instruct each person to place their two hands in front of them in a prayer-like manner (palms pressed together.)
2. Without moving any other fingers, move each of the middle fingers so that they cross side to side.
3. The middle fingers should be resting perpendicular to all other fingers.
4. Ensuring no other fingers cross, slide the palm of one hand away from the body while the middle fingers remain interlocked.
5. Keep sliding until the fingers of each hand partially overlap the palm of the other.
6. The middle fingers will be pointing in opposing directions on top of each other.
7. Now, wiggle these two extended middle fingers for fun.
8. After a few minutes of practice, invite each person to find a partner.
9. Starting with hands by their sides, on "GO" the first person to Wiggle Waggle, wins.

Variations

- In pairs, face one another, and set your arms and palms in the direction of the other. Place a palm each against your partners' two palms, and... um, you can guess the rest.
- Form a circle with each individual matching palms with their left and right-side neighbours. After a few moments of practice, time how long it takes from the arms-down position to achieve a full group Wiggle Waggle.

Reflection

- When you first started, how did you feel? Did this change with practice?
- In what ways did you observe people helping others?
- What might this exercise teach us about perseverance?

Toe To Toe

Challenging slow-motion balance exercise for partners.

Benefits

- Challenging
- Inspires critical-thinking
- Healthy competition
- Partner activity

People 2+

Time 1-2 mins

Instructions

1. Form pairs.
2. Ask a volunteer to step forward and place the toe of their right shoe directly in front of yours.
3. Then, as if standing on a straight line, place each of your left shoes directly behind the heel of your right shoes.
4. With each of your right toes touching, and using your right hands, engage in a hand-shake.
5. Aim of this exercise is to bring your partner off-balance.
6. All movements must be in 'slow-motion,' ie no sudden, jerky movements.
7. Play several rounds, and swap partners.

Variations

- Same exercise in reverse, with left feet toe to toe, and left hands clasped.
- Vary the distance between the toes of each person. The further they are apart, the more challenging it gets.

Reflection

- How balanced did you feel in the beginning? Did you improve?
- What was the most challenging part of the exercise?
- Were you tempted to move faster than slow-motion at times? Why?

Skipping Rope

Playful exercise to warm-up large groups quickly.

Benefits

- Quick & easy
- Playful & fun
- Inspires creativity
- Multiple variations

People 2+

Time 1-2 mins

Instructions

1. Use a wide-open space to give every person plenty of room to move.

2. Ask everyone to bend down and pick up an (imaginary) skipping rope placed in front of them.

3. By way of demonstration, step inside the rope and start rotating the rope over your body as if skipping, slowly at first, then increasing your pace.

4. Invite your group to follow your lead, as you demonstrate a wide variety of skipping rope moves, one after another, eg turn rope as many times in one jump, turn rope backwards, double-dutch, etc.

5. Continue for 1 to 2 minutes, or until you or your group is exhausted.

Variations

- Face another person who is skipping a few metres away, and toss your rope to them mid-skip as they toss theirs to you. Aim to keep your partner's rope spinning as you catch it.

- Ask your group to create and demonstrate some unique skipping rope moves.

Reflection

- How quickly did you feel a little exhausted?
- Which was the most enjoyable imaginary skipping move? Why?
- Can you think of more ways to rotate a skipping rope over your body?

Woodcutter's Warm-Up

Rapid & highly-energetic warm-up for two people.

Benefits

- Rapid warm-up
- Highly-energetic
- Demands collaboration
- Partner activity

People 2+

Time 1 min

Instructions

1. Find a partner.
2. Facing each other, each person holds the hands of their partner in a monkey-grip position, ie fingers curled inside the palm of partner.
3. Place one foot forward towards the other to establish a balanced stance.
4. Starting slowly, ask each person to begin to push their arms in and out, pumping back and forth alternately to their partner.
5. Gradually build up the pace and momentum until the pair cannot move their co-joined arms any faster.
6. Once out of breath, stop and let go.

Variations

- As above, crossing arms/hands with your partner.
- Form a tight circle of fellow lumberjacks or jills, and hold the hands of your two neighbours.

Reflection

- Were you surprised how quickly you warmed-up?
- What was necessary to develop a rhythm between you and your partner?
- Can you think of another area of your life that would benefit from developing a good rhythm?

Star Stretch

Inventive partner stretch to develop balance & trust.

Benefits

- Playful stretch
- Highly-interactive
- Builds agility & balance
- Develops trust

People 2+

Time 15-20 mins

Instructions

1. Form pairs
2. By way of demonstration, invite a volunteer to stand in front of you, feet together with approx 30cm between you and your partner's toes.
3. Grasp hands, and when comfortable, both lean back slowly with a straight body until each of your arms are straight.
4. Next, turn back to back and repeat the exercise, leaning forward away from your partner with arms behind you.
5. Finally, standing side-by-side and only holding the inside arm of your partner, lean away and lift your outside legs off the ground.
6. When balanced, slowly bring the soles of your outside feet to touch in front of your knees.
7. Repeat several times, and swap partners at regular intervals.

Variations

- As above, but one person starts facing the opposite direction of their partner. This time each person brings their own leg in front of their own bodies, aiming to touch the soles of their shoes inside the gap formed between their legs.
- Involve groups of three or four people. Often the most difficult part is finding a comfortable grip with one another, but otherwise, the physics works just the same.

Reflection

- What did you notice as the activity progressed? Did your balance improve? Why?
- What worked or did not work to achieve equilibrium with your partner?
- Are there any lessons from this exercise we could apply to our relationships?

Windmill Stretch

Challenging partner stretch that demands co-ordination.

Benefits

- Terrific stretch
- Challenging
- Promotes collaboration
- Partner activity

People 2+

Time 1-2 mins

Instructions

1. Find a partner of similar height, and stand back to back.
2. Each person extends their arms out to their sides, crossing arms slightly, applying pressure against their partner's palms.
3. With arms co-joined, start with a gentle rocking motion, up and down, up and down.
4. Once warmed-up, each pair brings one set of their arms over the tops of their heads, so that each person's elbows pass in front of their noses.
5. Continue to apply pressure to co-joined hands, as the arms continue in the same direction to eventually fold over to the other side of the body.
6. If both partners are comfortable, direct these arms down towards the ground and then poke the other arms up, over and through the gap created by the contorted arms.
7. Next, reverse the moves, untangle the arms, and repeat the process on the other side.
8. Building pace very slowly, go back and forth several times over 20 to 30 seconds.

Variations

- For less-agile groups, present only the first few steps of this exercise to enjoy the rocking back and forth motions only.
- For the very dexterous, invite pairs to move their feet in the direction of where they have pointed their arms, effectively turning themselves inside-out and back again several times.

Reflection

- What parts of your body did you feel stretch the most during this exercise?
- How hard was it for you to constantly apply pressure to your partner's hands?
- Did you achieve a certain rhythm in your movements? How did that feel?

Gotcha

Quick, simple & hilarious energiser for all group sizes.

Benefits

- Extremely fun
- Spontaneous laughter
- Sharpens reflexes
- Any size group

People 2+

Time 2-5 mins

Instructions

1. Form a circle, including yourself, facing inwards and standing side by side.
2. Everyone holds their right hand palm-facing up towards their right-hand side neighbour.
3. Everyone places the end of their left pointer finger into the open palm of their left-hand neighbour.
4. On "GO" everyone attempts to catch the finger of their partner in their right palm while also avoiding their finger being caught by their left-hand neighbour.
5. A person who successfully catches a finger in their palm yells "GOTCHA!"
6. Repeat several times.
7. If time permits, try or invent a variation.

Variations

- Cross your arms as you play, ie extend the right palm towards the person on your left, and place your left index finger into the waiting palm on your right.
- Start with pairs, play a few rounds or variations, and then combine with another pair to make a group of four. Four then becomes eight, and so on until everyone is part of one large circle.

Reflection

- Was it easy to do two things at the same time? Why or why not?
- What skills do you think are sharpened or developed in this exercise?
- How might this activity reflect our group?

People To People

Anatomical pairing game with lots of fun movements.

Benefits

- Very playful
- Highly-interactive
- Promotes collaboration
- Partner activity

People 8+

Time 5-10 mins

Instructions

1. Form pairs, standing in a circle around you in the middle.
2. Initiate a beat by clapping your hands, and invite your group to follow your lead for a few moments.
3. Explain that during the beat, you will call the names of any two body parts, eg "NOSE & ELBOW."
4. On this command, each person turns to their partner and touches one part of the announced anatomy to the other anatomical part belonging to their partner.
5. Everyone repeats the names of the body parts as they keep the beat.
6. Upon completing this task, everyone resumes their clapping, awaiting the next command.
7. Continue this routine several times, until the command "PEOPLE TO PEOPLE" is randomly called, at which point, everyone seeks a new partner.
8. The person who is left without a partner, resumes the role of the person calling from the middle.
9. Play several rounds, or try a variation.

Variations

- Invite everyone to mix and mingle with the rest of the group, until randomly an anatomical call is made, at which point everyone must find any partner to match the prescribed body parts.
- Form groups of three or four people. If more than one person ends up in the middle, ask these people to share the calling of anatomical parts and join the matching action together.

Reflection

- What was your favourite anatomical match? Why?
- Were some body parts harder to match or touch than others? Why?
- How fast did you move when "PEOPLE TO PEOPLE" was called? Why?

Freeze Frame

Active energiser that works powerfully as an initiative.

Benefits

- Simple
- Active
- Non-threatening
- Fosters collaboration

People 8+

Time 5-10 mins

Instructions

1. Ask your group to spread themselves evenly throughout a large open area.

2. Invite everyone to walk aimlessly and silently about the area.

3. After approx 10 seconds has elapsed, any one or more individuals may choose to freeze and stop walking.

4. Anyone who spots another person who has frozen is invited to freeze immediately too.

5. Time how long it takes for the whole group to freeze, ie from the moment the first person freezes to the last person.

6. Aim to record the quickest time to freeze the whole group.

7. Allow many rounds, inviting the group to improve their performance (time.)

Variations

- After several of the introductory rounds, ask your group to increase the speed of their mingling, and then in a later round, add sharp, random turns in direction.

- As above, and permit very brisk walking (not quite a jog or run) if you believe your group has a good level of safety-consciousness to keep their movements safe, especially with the sharp corners.

Reflection

- Did your group continuously improve its time with each round? How did this happen?

- What was required to get the whole group to freeze?

- How might what was required to be successful in this exercise relate to your work, school, sport, etc?

Fill The Space

Active energiser featuring lead & follow interactions.

Benefits

- Simple
- Playful & fun
- Ideal for large groups
- Develops critical-thinking

People 12+

Time 2-5 mins

Instructions

1. Ask your group to spread evenly throughout a large, open area.

2. Invite everyone to walk aimlessly and silently about the area.

3. Loudly announce that you would like everyone to secretly identify one other person who is presently situated on the other side of the area.

4. Each person aims to follow behind this 'secret' person as closely as possible, without being noticed.

5. After 10 to 20 seconds, ask the group to resume their aimless mingling.

6. Repeat the process with a new secret admirer, and/or introduce a variation.

Variations

- For each individual, identify a secret person close by, and then aim to keep as far away as possible (within the boundaries) from this person.

- For each individual, identify a secret person on other side of the area, then aim to keep an equal distance in front of this person at all times. As a further twist, encourage everyone to ensure that their secret person notices them.

Reflection

- What feelings did you experience during the activity?
- How difficult was it to go 'un-noticed?'
- What did this exercise remind you of in 'real-life?'

Mission Impossible

Quick, fun & chaotic 'cat-and-mouse' style energiser.

Benefits

- Simple
- Playful & fun
- Ideal for large groups
- Develops critical-thinking

People 12+

Time 1-2 mins

Instructions

1. Ask your group to spread evenly throughout a large, open area.

2. Everyone secretly identifies two other people in the group.

3. Each person aims to keep one of the secret people directly between themselves and the other secret person at all times.

4. Stop after 20 to 30 seconds, and repeat with two new secret people.

Variations

- Identify two 'secret' people. Each person forms an imaginary line between themselves and one of the secret people, and moves quickly to keep prevent the second secret person from 'crossing' that line.

- Take a look at **Fill The Space** to explore a similar chaotic energiser game.

Reflection

- Did you enjoy the chaos, or not? Why?

- How difficult was it to maintain a straight line between you and your two secret people?

- What did this exercise remind you of in 'real-life?'

Count Off

Mesmerising group energiser that is challenging & fun.

Benefits

- Quick & simple
- Ideal time-filler
- Requires concentration
- Triggers spontaneous laughter

People 8+

Time 1-2 mins

Instructions

1. Assemble your group within hearing range of one another.

2. Group aims to count from one to twenty, with three conditions:
   - Each person is entitled to only call one number at a time;
   - Any time two or more people call out a number at the same time, the count returns to zero; and
   - No pattern, sequence or directions may be given to indicate whose turn is next.

3. Start by calling "ONE" yourself, inviting your group to respond.

4. Allow many attempts over the course of 1 to 2 minutes, or until interest begins to wane.

Variations

- Ask your group to close their eyes as they count off during the activity.
- Choose any list to recite, such as the alphabet, chemical tables, months of the year, and numbers of seven (eg 7, 14, 17, 21, 27, 28, etc.)

Reflection

- How did you feel as the count off got closer to 20?
- Do you think this task is possible? Why or why not?
- What signs do you look for to know that someone is about to speak?

Ro Sham Bo

Inclusive & energetic variation of Rock-Paper-Scissors.

Benefits

- Quick & simple
- Highly-interactive
- Friendly competition
- Multiple variations

People 8+

Time 2-5 mins

Instructions

1. Establish a standard 'Rock-Paper-Scissors' protocol for your group.

2. In pairs, each person engages their partner in a quick game, eg each person calls "ONE, TWO, THREE" and then shoots.

3. Rock beats scissors, scissors beat paper, and paper beats rock. A tie means play another round.

4. The 'winner' invites the 'loser' to stand behind them, with hands on shoulders, forming a conga-line behind the winner.

5. Process continues with 'losers' joining the winning conga-line, until there are two long conga-lines remaining.

6. Invite a final show-down, and applaud the 'winners.'

7. Repeat by suddenly announcing "GO."

Variations

- When a person 'loses' they step behind their 'winning' partner and become part of a large, noisy cheer squad. These fans clap, shout and do whatever they like to show their undying support, until their 'leader' loses a round, at which point they all immediately switch loyalty.

- Every time a person or conga-line wins, all existing members of the line turn to face 180 degrees the other direction and invite the 'loser' (either an individual or entire conga-line of people, headed by the defeated person) to be their new leader.

Reflection

- Do you have a strategy for winning 'Rock-Paper-Scissors?'
- How did it feel to lose, but then join the winning team?
- Which is more important – to win, or enjoy playing?

ESP

Exciting partner activity that explores working together.

Benefits

- Highly-interactive
- Non-threatening
- Inspires powerful metaphors
- Promotes collaboration

People 2+

Time 10-15 mins

Instructions

1. Form into pairs.
2. Identify three definable and unique physical gestures which reflect your program goals, or any three things such as Happy, Sad and Shocked.
3. Practice all three gestures several times with your group.
4. Pairs start by standing back to back with their partners.
5. On the count of three, everyone turns around swiftly to face their partner while demonstrating one of the three gestures.
6. Each person aims to match the gesture of their partner as often as possible within, say, five rounds.

Variations

- Introduce any three connected 'things' such as Hollywood icons, emotions, objects, seasons, etc.
- Use as a fun way to introduce an important component of your program, eg a working agreement whereby you create a distinct physical gesture for each element.

Reflection

- How could you successfully match your partner's gestures more often?
- Could you or your group benefit from communicating more effectively? How? Describe one example?
- What is necessary to ensure that everyone in your group or team is 'on the same page?'

Quick Line-Up

Energetic, large group energiser
for wide, open spaces.

Benefits

- Playful & fun
- Highly-energetic
- Inspires collaboration
- Demands critical-thinking

People 12+

Time 2-5 mins

Instructions

1. Form four teams of roughly even numbers.
2. Standing in the middle of an open space, the members of each team stand in a straight line to represent one (or four) sides of a square.
3. Position yourself in the middle of this square.
4. Facing towards one of the teams, ask each team to acknowledge their position relative to you, eg front, back, left or right.
5. When you shift your position, every team must re-orient themselves, so that they return to their original orientation relative to you.
6. On the call "QUICK LINE-UP" each team must re-orient themselves, re-form their line, hold hands and say "WE'RE HERE" as quickly as possible.
7. The team which re-positions itself the quickest, wins that round.
8. Play several rounds, during which you move progressively further from your group.

Variations

- Instruct each team to perform a physical task, such as three star-jumps or push-ups, prior to re-aligning themselves.
- Ask 2 to 4 people to stand evenly throughout the space with responsibility for randomly calling "QUICK LINE-UP," although only one at a time. First team to re-position themselves correctly around the caller wins that round.

Reflection

- Did you take any short-cuts to achieve a rapid line-up? In what way?
- What was the most challenging part of this exercise?
- What helped your group successfully line-up?

Shipwreck

Fun, suspenseful & highly-energetic large group game.

Benefits

- Highly-energetic
- Sharpens reflex skills
- Sharpens listening skills
- Multiple variations

People 12+

Time 10-15 mins

Instructions

1. Gather your group in the centre of the playing space, and ask them to imagine they are standing on the deck of a tall-ship.
2. Indicate where the bow, stern, port and starboard positions of the ship are.
3. When you call a command, each person is expected to respond as quickly as possible, eg move to the stern.
4. In addition to instructing your group to move to the "BOW," "STERN," "PORT" and "STARBOARD" positions, other calls may include:
   - "ATTENTION" – individuals stand to attention, saluting with their right hand.
   - "SWAB THE DECK" – individuals get on their hands and knees and scrub the deck.
   - "LIFEBOATS" – three people form a single file line, sit down and pretend to row a boat.
   - "RIG THE SAILS" – two people join hands and pretend to be setting up the sails.
5. Start the game by making your first of a series of commands in quick succession, waiting a few moments between each command.
6. Continue for several minutes, or try a variation.

Variations

- Eliminate people when (a) one or more sailors are the last to perform a particular task or (b) one or more sailors can not form a complete team to perform the chore.
- Call "SAILOR OVERBOARD" to instruct everyone still on deck to rescue an eliminated sailor.

Reflection

- What did you notice as you attempted to respond to all of the commands?
- What was necessary to help you respond successfully to each command?
- Where else in your life do you need to respond quickly and accurately?

Salt & Pepper

Simple call-and-response large group energiser.

Benefits

- Simple
- Energetic
- Sharpens reflexes
- Sharpens listening skills

People 8+

Time 5-10 mins

Instructions

1. Ask everyone in your group to stand to one side of a long line marked on the ground.

2. Encourage people to spread themselves evenly along the line, within 30cm of the line.

3. Identify one side of the line as 'Salt' and the other as 'Pepper.'

4. Loudly announce a series of calls such as "SALT, PEPPER, SALT, SALT..."

5. Immediately upon each call, each person must jump to the correct side.

6. If an individual makes an error, eg jumps to the wrong side of the line, they are eliminated.

7. Each person aims to stay in the game for as long as possible.

8. The last person remaining wins.

Variations

- Form into pairs, and instruct all moves must now be made with a partner (often facing each other and holding hands.) If one or both partners make an error, then they are both eliminated.

- Mark two parallel lines on the ground (placed about 60cm apart) to create three areas for your group to jump in and out of. To be fair, the caller can only call the name of a directly adjacent side for people to jump into.

Reflection

- What did you notice about yourself or others as the activity progressed?
- What did you say to yourself when you happened to make a wrong move?
- What strategies did you employ to help you focus on making the right moves?

Around The World

Fun, whole-of-group maths energiser.

Benefits

- Very active
- Healthy competition
- Small or large groups
- Multiple variations

People 8+

Time 2-5 mins

Instructions

1. To begin, present a few rounds of **Your Add** to warm-up your group.

2. Within a large, open playing space, designate three or four areas as belonging to well-known cities or countries of the world, eg New York, Tokyo, Sydney, etc.

3. Each person moves to the city or country that they'd like to visit most.

4. Each person aims to travel to each of the designated cities or countries in a clockwise direction as often as possible within two minutes.

5. To move from one city or country to the next, a person must win a quick game of **Your Add** involving any person standing in the same area.

6. The 'winner' is permitted to advance clockwise to the next city, while the 'loser' will remain in the same area and will play **Your Add** with a new person.

7. The person who completes the most number of rotations (of all areas) within the allotted time is declared the winner.

Variations

- Each person is given a card from a deck of playing cards. When two people meet, they present their cards and the first person to call the sum of the two cards, wins. Picture cards – Jack, Queen, King – are valued at 10 points each. Ace can be valued at 1 or 11.

- When two people meet, they each roll a die. The first person to announce the correct sum, wins and gets to move forward.

Reflection

- How many rotations of the 'world' did you accomplish? What does this mean?
- How did it feel to win/lose several rounds in a row? What did you tell yourself?
- What strategies did you employ to help you win? Was this fair?

I've Got The Power

Creative large group stretching & mimicking exercise.

Benefits

- Very playful
- Highly-energetic
- Inspires creativity
- All group sizes

People 8+

Time   2-5 mins

Instructions

1. Form a circle, facing into the centre, including yourself.
2. Invite a volunteer to perform a fun, quirky movement or stretch.
3. Once introduced, the rest of the group is asked to mimic that movement as best they can.
4. The volunteer continues their movement for 5 to 10 seconds, and then invites a new person to introduce the next movement.
5. Continue this routine multiple times around the group.

Variations

- One person starts with a really small, barely noticeable movement (eg blinking their eyes several times,) then the next person is obliged to present a really large make-you-sweat movement (eg jogging on the spot raising knees as high as they can.) Then back to a micro movement again, and so on.
- Introduce an imaginary prop, such as a hula-hoop, piece of rope, bowling ball, to be somehow involved in the stretch. The mimicry of the group continues.

Reflection

- Was it hard to think of an interesting stretch?
- What did it feel like to have the rest of the group mimic your actions?
- Ordinarily, what do we think when people mimic our actions?

Wave Stretch

Whole group wave-like stretch with fun, quirky movements.

Benefits

- Simple
- Highly-energetic
- Inspires creativity
- Fosters patience

People 8+

Time 2-5 mins

Instructions

1. Form a circle facing into the centre, including yourself.

2. Initiate a quirky movement or stretch, and ask that it is quickly mimicked by everyone else, one person at a time in a clock-wise direction around the circle.

3. When everybody is performing your movement, you continue to doing it while your left-hand neighbour introduces a new movement.

4. The new movement is mimicked all the way around the circle, and finally adopted by you when it passes you.

5. Continue this routine for several minutes.

Variations

- Once a particular stretch returns to the person who introduced it, invite any person anywhere in the circle, to introduce the next stretch for the group to mimic.

- Send a 'wave' of two movements or stretches at the same time, in different directions. Once the two movements return from whence they came, a new person initiates a move. There'll be total chaos, but tons of fun.

Reflection

- Did you forget to keep doing your own stretch when it returned to you? Why?
- What was the reaction of the group to your 'mistake?' Is this response typical?
- What's necessary to create an atmosphere in which mistakes are okay?

Yurt Circle

Whole-group stretch & initiative based on traditional yurt.

Benefits

- Powerful stretch
- Promotes collaboration
- Develops critical-thinking
- Values diversity

People 8+

Time 2-5 mins

Instructions

1. Form a perfect circle, facing into centre.
2. Everyone firmly grasps the hands of their neighbours.
3. Step back slowly, to stretch the circle outwards, so that people's arms are almost parallel to the ground.
4. With feet placed together and securely planted on the ground, ask your group to slowly lean backwards.
5. Instruct people to adjust the position of their feet, so that when they lean backwards they feel fully supported.
6. Aim to maintain this self-supported stance for as long as possible, before regaining one's balance.
7. Repeat several times, or try a variation.

Variations

- Form multiple small groups of four to ten people, perhaps then building up to involve the whole group.
- With an even number of people, ask that every second person leans in on "GO" while every other person leans out of the circle. Once equilibrium is reached, ask that their positions are (slowly) swapped from their current stance.

Reflection

- To achieve a strong, fully supported balance, what did you need to do, or adjust?
- How did it feel when you achieved this balance?
- How might this exercise teach us some lessons about how successful relationships work?

Knee Impulse

Quick & simple circle energiser
to fill-in a few minutes.

Benefits

- Passive
- Playful & fun
- Fosters trust & empathy
- Ideal time-filler

People 8+

Time 2-5 mins

Instructions

1. Form a circle in a way that brings everyone's legs (knees) close to their neighbours.
2. Everyone extends their arms out in front, palms facing down.
3. Place your left hand on your left-side neighbour's knee, and right hand on your right-side neighbour's knee, ie all arms are crossed with their neighbours.
4. To start, one person taps one of their hands on a neighbour's knee to initiate a series of taps.
5. The impulse travels from left to right in sequence of the group's knees.
6. Your group aims to tap all knees in sequence around the circle as quickly as possible.
7. Repeat several times, then reverse direction.

Variations

- Send the impulse both directions at the same time, by simultaneously tapping your left- and right-side neighbour's knees. The impulses will have to cross somewhere near the half-way point of the circle before returning to you.
- When someone taps their hand two times in rapid succession – tap-tap – the direction of the impulse reverses. If someone taps in error (ie where they anticipated the direction would not change, but it did,) that person is asked to remove their hand from the game. Game continues until you are left with the hands of only three contestants.

Reflection

- How did you feel when you were first asked to place your hands on the knees of another person?
- How difficult was it for you to maintain the correct sequence of hand taps?
- Where else in our lives do we find it difficult to keep to a sequence?

Chic-A-Boom

Entertaining large group energiser.

Benefits

- Playful & fun
- Ideal for large-groups
- Highly-interactive
- Fosters creativity

People 12+

Time 2-5 mins

Instructions

1. Form a large circle, including yourself.
2. Demonstrate a series of moves, asking your group to copy you, pointing your index fingers alternately up and down, and to the left and right.
3. Teach them the following chorus, making the appropriate moves with each line:
   "....AAAAND, UP CHIC-A-BOOM, CHIC-A-BOOM, CHIC-A-BOOM.
   AND DOWN CHIC-A-BOOM, CHIC-A-BOOM, CHIC-A-BOOM.
   TO THE LEFT, CHIC-A-BOOM, CHIC-A-BOOM, CHIC-A-BOOM.
   TO THE RIGHT, CHIC-A-BOOM, CHIC-A-BOOM, CHIC-A-BOOM."
4. You move into middle of circle singing this tune as you look directly at one person:
   "HEY THERE [enter name,] YOU'RE A REAL COOL CAT.
   YOU'VE GOTTA LOT OF THIS, AND YOU'VE GOTTA LOT OF THAT.
   SO COME ON IN AND GET DOWN......"
5. At this point, invite this volunteer into the centre of the circle with you.
6. Resume singing the chorus, inviting the whole group to sing it with you.
7. When chorus is sung, each person in middle invites someone new to join in centre.
8. This chorus and verse routine continues until everyone ends up in the centre of the circle, for one final rendition of the chorus.

Variation

- Alter some of the lyrics or dance moves!

Reflection

- How did you first feel when someone invited you into the centre of the circle?
- How did you feel at the end, when everyone was dancing in the middle?
- Where else in your life does 'strength in numbers' make a difference to you?

Use the QR code reader of your smart phone to bring the activities alive

You can browse many of the activities for free, or choose to subscribe to unlock tons of premium content

CHAPTER 11
Tag & Running Games

This section features games and exercises which are ideal for physical education (PE) classes and any group that has plenty of energy to spare, or simply want to enjoy the wild abandon of a good chase.

Although primarily fun, tag activities are useful as warm-up exercises as much as they provide a setting for your group to take some risks, eg exert energy, run around like a fool and touch others in a safe environment.

Activities in which physical activity is a significant element typically feature:

- Fun as a major component
- Mix of inclusive and elimination-style structures
- Ability for individuals to choose their level of involvement
- Emphasis on physical movement and interaction
- Focus on participation rather than win or lose
- 1 to 20 minutes of play

Partners

Toe Tag – Snoopy & Red Baron – Finger Fencing – Knee Tag – Hip Tag

Whole Group

Triangle Tag – Elbow Tag – Walk Tag – Blob Tag – Head-Butt Tag
Hug Tag – Giants Wizards Elves – Everybody Is It – Hospital Tag
Dead Ant Tag – Basketball Court Tag – Name Tag

Toe Tag

Hilarious, high-energy tag game for two people.

Benefits

- Highly-energetic
- Quick warm-up
- Ideal time-filler
- Partner activity

People 2+

Time   1-2 mins

Instructions

1. Form into pairs.

2. Start by standing back to back with your partner.

3. On "GO" each person spins around to face their partner and attempts to 'tag' the other's toes.

4. A person scores a point for being the first to make a successful tag.

5. Play several rounds, first to earn three points wins.

Variations

- Start by facing your partner and holding his or her hands. While this set-up will eliminate the need to chase your partner, beware that heads may clash as all of the focus is on the feet.

- Form a circle with four or five people. Each person attempts to tag the feet of their immediate left- and right-hand neighbours. As soon as a person has had both feet tagged, they are eliminated. The circle re-joins and the game continues until the final two people face-off in a championship duel.

Reflection

- What strategies did you employ to avoid being tagged?
- What strategies did you employ to make a tag?
- Was the game 'safe?' If not, why not?

Snoopy & Red Baron

*Novel & energetic partner stretch
& tagging exercise.*

Benefits

- Playful stretch
- Highly-energetic
- Healthy competition
- Partner activity

People 2+

Time 1-2 mins

Instructions

1. Form pairs.
2. Each person stands facing their partner about half-metre apart and places both hands into their pockets (or behind their back.)
3. Nominate one person as the Red Baron (chaser) and the other as Snoopy (the chased.)
4. When ready, each person removes one hand from their pocket and manoeuvres their hand to either avoid or make contact with their partner's hand.
5. When contact is made, swap roles.
6. Play several rounds and/or swap partners.

Variations

- Each person is entitled to use both hands, giving each of them twice the chance of air-borne success.
- Rather than compete, invite one person to follow closely behind the hand of their partner, almost as if they were two swallows or swifts. Hands never touch, but the hand which follows aims to keep as close as possible, matching the exact moves of their counterpart.

Reflection

- How difficult was it to follow your partner's movements?
- How did it feel when you and your partner were in sync?
- What muscles in particular did you use the most?

Finger Fencing

Dynamic & physically challenging tagging game for pairs.

Benefits

- Playful & fun
- Highly-energetic
- Physically challenging
- Partner activity

People 2+

Time 1-2 mins

Instructions

1. Form pairs.

2. Each person grasps the right hand of their partner in a special handshake whereby each of their thumbs rests on top of their partner's hand.

3. Each person extends and points their index finger towards their partner, creating a 'foil.'

4. On the call of "ON GUARD," each person aims to be the first to tag their partner somewhere below their waist, ie with the end of their finger.

5. Play several rounds, or swap partners.

Variations

- Designate a tight boundary inside which the action can take place. If someone steps outside the boundary, they are considered tagged.

- While attempting to tag your opponent with your finger, try to tag one of their feet with your foot as well.

Reflection

- What did you discover as you started to engage with your partner?
- How difficult was it for you to either evade a tag, or make a tag?
- What specific skills did you use to play successfully?

Knee Tag

*Fun, high-energy tag game
for pairs & large groups.*

Benefits

- Simple
- Very energetic
- Highly-interactive
- Partner activity

People 2+

Time 2-5 mins

Instructions

1. Form pairs.
2. Standing with their feet about shoulder-width apart, each person faces their partner and places their hands on their own knees.
3. Each person attempts to touch the unguarded knee of their partner as often as possible to score a point.
4. After 20 seconds, the person with the most points wins.
5. Start a new round, swap partners, or try a variation.

Variations

- Allow individuals to move and the ability to tag any undefended knees belonging to any person moving about them.
- Call "HANDS UP" to cause everyone to hold their hands above their heads and not ever defend their knees. They may, of course, choose to lower a hand to make a committed tag of any exposed knees. Shortly after, call "HANDS DOWN" to allow people once again guard their knees, until the next "HANDS UP" and so on.

Reflection

- Were you successful? How do you define your success?
- Did you have fun? Why or why not?
- Did you observe any behaviours which concerned you?

Hip Tag

Fun partner exercise to teach the value of collaboration.

Benefits

- Simple
- Quick execution
- Promotes collaboration
- Partner activity

People 2+

Time 1-2 mins

Instructions

1. Form pairs.
2. Standing side by side with their partner, hold hands.
3. When ready, each person aims to touch the back of their partner's hand against their own hip as many times as possible.
4. Stop the activity after 10 to 15 seconds has elapsed.
5. If useful, survey individual scores, and invite your group to reflect on the range of results.

Variation

- Present the activity to two (physically separate) groups. The first group is instructed as above, while the second group (whom can not hear or see the first group engage) is given perhaps a more collaborative briefing. Excellent opportunity to reflect on the difference our language can make.

Reflection

- What did you hear or think when the activity was first introduced to you?
- How did you define success? Why?
- Which result was better – a low competitive score or a large collaborative score? Why?

Triangle Tag

Extremely fun chasing exercise for groups of four people.

Benefits

- Quick warm-up
- Highly-energetic
- Promotes collaboration
- Challenging

People 4+

Time 1-2 mins

Instructions

1. Form groups of four people.
2. Ask three of the four to form a triangle by holding hands.
3. Designate one of these three people to be the initial target.
4. When ready, the fourth person aims to move on the outside of the triangle to tag the target.
5. All moves & tags must be made outside of the triangle.
6. Once a tag is made, or 30 seconds has elapsed, invite everyone to swap roles.

Variations

- Form a triangle by holding onto shoulders rather than hands, ie makes it slightly easier for the tagger.
- Use four people to form the, um… triangle. Ideal challenge for very athletic groups.

Reflection

- What did you quickly learn as you started to play this game?
- How difficult was it for you to either evade the tagger, or make a tag?
- What specific skills did you use to play successfully?

Elbow Tag

Fast-paced whole of group tag game with many surprises.

Benefits

- Very fun
- Highly-energetic
- Interactive
- Promotes critical-thinking

People 8+

Time 2-5 mins

Instructions

1. Forms pairs.
2. Link arms or elbows with partner, and place outside hands on hips.
3. Position pairs randomly throughout the playing space, not too close to other pairs.
4. Nominate one pair to uncouple, and assume the role of 'cat' and 'mouse.'
5. The 'cat' will chase the 'mouse' around the stationary pairs attempting to tag them.
6. If a tag is made, roles immediately reverse.
7. During the chase, the 'mouse' is permitted to link arms with any other person to escape the 'cat.'
8. Linking with a person will cause their partner to be unlinked and released into the chase as the new 'mouse.'
9. Introduce more cats and mice into the action as appropriate.

Variations

- Permit the 'cat' to also seek shelter with a linked-pair at any time, and in so doing, create a new cat.
- To avoid a terminally long reign as a cat (or mouse) announce that if a tag or link is not made within ten seconds (or 20 steps, etc) the roles of the cat and mouse automatically reverse.

Reflection

- Did you prefer to be the cat or the mouse? Why?
- Were you taken by surprise at any point in the game? What happened?
- Were there any behaviours that you observed which concerned you?

Walk Tag

*Ideal partner tag exercise
for limited spaces.*

Benefits

- Simple
- Ideal for small spaces
- Highly-interactive
- Develops critical-thinking

People 8+

Time 2-5 mins

Instructions

1. Form pairs.
2. Designate an area of approx 5m x 5m in which to play.
3. Instruct everyone to enter and play only in this space.
4. For each pair, identify who will be the first tagger.
5. Everyone assumes the Bumpers Up position, ie palms facing forward in front of chest.
6. On "GO" all taggers must spin 720 degrees on the spot before they can chase their partner.
7. All movement must be made by walking, no running permitted.
8. Instruct everyone to avoid contact with any other person during the course of the chase.
9. Once a tag is made, the partners switch roles, and the new tagger will spin around twice on the spot.
10. Play several rounds, or until the energy of your group starts to wane.

Variations

- Ask partners to physically connect with each other (by way of hands or linked arms) and chase another nominated coupled-pair. Note, partners may only travel around others.
- Make the boundaries very close, but still permitting movement and drop the rule regarding 'no contact with any other person.' If a heightened level of safety consciousness has been developed in the earlier rounds, you can expect fewer 'safety issues' will arise.

Reflection

- What helped you to make a successful tag, or avoid being tagged?
- As the space got smaller, were you less or more successful?
- What did you notice about the level of safety-consciousness during the game?

Blob Tag

Very energetic, ever-expanding, co-operative tag game.

Benefits

- Highly-energetic
- Ideal for large areas
- Promotes collaboration
- Develops critical-thinking

People 12+

Time 5-10 mins

Instructions

1. Form pairs, with each pair holding hands.
2. Invite one pair to start as the 'blob' or initial tagging team.
3. All other pairs spread throughout a wide, open designated area.
4. All pairs must hold hands at all times. If a fleeing pair release hands, they will be deemed to have been tagged.
5. Upon being tagged, a pair will release hands and, as individuals, assume a tagging position at each end of the blob, before resuming the chase.
6. If two or more people forming part of the blob lose grip, the blob can not successfully tag a fleeing pair until re-joined.
7. Game continues until the last pair has been tagged.

Variations

- Allow the blob to stop at anytime, release their holds and switch 180 degrees to rejoin and resume their chase for purposes of strategy and convenience.
- If working with a mixed group, challenge them to 'save' any one pair which consists of an X-Y combination (for example, girl and boy) to make it possible to re-populate the X-Y world at the end. In this case, the blob will need to be very intentional about which pairs they choose to chase and tag.

Reflection

- What strategies did you employ to avoid being tagged?
- As the blob, what worked and what didn't work to help you tag other pairs?
- At what point did the game reach a 'tipping point' ie when the odds switched in favour of the blob?

Head-Butt Tag

Highly-energetic tag game with ever-changing teams.

Benefits

- Simple
- Fast-paced
- Chaotic fun
- Promotes collaboration

People 8+

Time 2-5 mins

Instructions

1. Spread group evenly throughout a wide, open space.
2. On the count of three, everyone will choose to place their hands on either their head or bottom.
3. This choice will determine the team they initially belong to.
4. Members of the heads team aim to tag those on the butts team, and vice versa.
5. When a tag is made, the person who is tagged immediately switches teams.
6. Game continues until everyone belongs to the same team.

Variations

- Individuals may place their hands on any part of their upper torso, eg tummy, shoulder, ears, back, etc. When a tag is made, the person will adopt the look of the person who just tagged them. Note, that as there are likely to be many more team variants, the game will continue for much longer.
- Create three even teams - Rock (place hands on head,) Paper (hands on hips) and Scissors (arms crossed on chest.) Once the game starts, Rocks can tag (beat) Scissors, Scissors can tag Papers and Papers can tag Rocks. Once tagged, that person switches teams. Game continues until everyone is on the same team.

Reflection

- What strategies did you employ to stay in the game as long as possible?
- Did you work with others on your team to tag your opponents?
- How did it feel to change teams when you got tagged? Did you resist, even a tiny bit?

Hug Tag

Highly-interactive tag game that rewards human touch.

Benefits

- Playful & fun
- Highly-energetic
- Promotes collaboration
- Powerful metaphor

People 12+

Time 2-5 mins

Instructions

1. Spread your group evenly throughout a designated area.
2. Nominate a volunteer to be the initial tagger, ie they will soon start chasing others.
3. In an effort to avoid being tagged, an individual may choose to run very fast, or engage in a mutual hug with another person.
4. Two people may only embrace in a hug for three seconds, after which they must separate and return to the game.
5. The 'tagger' is not entitled to hover over hugging pairs.
6. When a tag is made, the roles reverse and the new 'tagger' resumes the chase.
7. Continue play for several minutes, or until your group's energy starts to wane.

Variations

- Particularly for large groups, introduce two or more 'taggers' to increase the energy and interaction of the game.
- Explain that a 'safe' hug can only occur between two parties of the same or different (depending on your goals) teams, genders, nationalities, family, clothing colour, etc. This parameter may open the possibility of an interesting conversation once the game is finished.

Reflection

- What was it like to seek refuge in the arms of another person?
- What decisions did you make directly prior to engaging in a hug? Was it spontaneous, planned, begrudged, etc?
- When was the last time you asked for help? Was this difficult to do?

Giants Wizards Elves

Playful whole-of-group tag game with ever-changing teams.

Benefits

- Very playful & fun
- Highly-energetic
- Promotes collaboration
- Inspires creativity

People 12+

Time 15-20 mins

Instructions

1. Mark two 'safe' areas approx 30 metres apart, with a line situated in the middle.

2. Divide your group into two teams.

3. Ask your group to mimic your actions as you establish three distinct physical characters:
   - Giants: Arms held high above your head, calling 'ROOOAAARRR.'
   - Wizards: Arms and fingers extended forward as if casting a spell, saying "ZZZZZZZ."
   - Elves: Bent knees and hold your ears, squeaking "ELF, ELF ELF."

4. Explain that Giants chase Wizards, Wizards chase Elves and Elves chase Giants.

5. Each team huddles in their safe area to agree on Plan A character and Plan B character.

6. When ready, both teams stand in middle facing one another about 2 metres apart.

7. On your count of "1, 2, 3" each team reveals their (Plan A) character. If two different characters are revealed, one team chases the other back to their zone.

8. If a person is tagged before they reach their safe zone, they switch teams.

9. If each team reveals the same character, they prepare to reveal their Plan B character.

10. Play several rounds until one team wins everyone on their side.

Variations

- Create three different characters, eg fox, chicken and human-being!
- Replace the three characters with the standard actions of Rock, Paper and Scissors.

Reflection

- What process did your team adopt to decide which character it would play?
- How did it feel to suddenly join another team?
- Generally speaking, how difficult is it for you to accept change? Why?

Everybody Is It

All-time classic, large group tag game, with twists.

Benefits

- Simple
- Rapid execution
- Highly-interactive
- Develops critical-thinking

People 8+

Time 2-5 mins

Instructions

1. Spread your group throughout a designated area.
2. When you call "GO" everyone attempts to tag everyone else, while also working hard to avoid being tagged.
3. When tagged, a person is obliged to simply crouch down and wait.
4. Briefly acknowledge the 'winner,' and then call "GO" again.

Variations

- In the moment of contest, if a person takes a backward step, they are deemed 'out.' Ruthless, I know!
- Take a look at **Hospital Tag** to play a more enduring version of this classic tag and to explore two further variations.

Reflection

- Did this activity evoke any memories of tag games when you were younger?
- What strategies did you employ to stay in the game for as long as possible?
- Was the game fun, and if not, why not?

Hospital Tag

Creative & highly-energetic tag game for large groups.

Benefits

- Simple
- Highly-interactive
- Fun variation of classic tag
- Develops critical-thinking

People 8+

Time 2-5 mins

Instructions

1. Spread your group throughout a designated area.

2. When you call "GO" everyone attempts to tag everyone else, while also working hard to avoid being tagged.

3. The first and second time a person is tagged, they are obliged to place a hand on the spot they are tagged.

4. Upon being tagged twice, a person may use their hips to tag others.

5. Upon being tagged a third time, a person is obliged to crouch down and wait.

6. Play two or more rounds over several minutes, or until the energy wanes.

Variations

- Entitle each person to more or less than three lives, regardless of the number of hands they possess.

- A crouched-down 'out' person may tag the passing feet and legs of those who are still in the game (note, only tags are permitted, no grabbing.) This action will cause the tagged person to go 'out' and entitle the tagger to return to the action. This gives the game even more longevity.

Reflection

- Was this game fun? Why or why not?

- What does being eliminated early or late in the game say to you? Why?

- Did you observe any behaviours or actions that concerned you during the game?

Dead Ant Tag

Zany & highly-interactive tag game for large groups.

Benefits

- Very playful & fun
- Highly-interactive
- Promotes collaboration
- Ideal for large groups

People 12+

Time 2-5 mins

Instructions

1. Randomly identify a series of small areas within a wide, open space, naming them 'ant hospitals.'
2. Spread your group throughout this space and announce that they are all 'ants.'
3. One person volunteers to be 'It' and attempts to tag as many people as possible.
4. When someone is tagged, they must drop to the ground, with arms and legs wiggling in the air, and call out "DEAD ANT, DEAD ANT..." until they are saved.
5. Grabbing one limb each, four other ants may carry a dead ant to the closest ant hospital.
6. A person assisting a dead ant (by holding a limb) is safe from being tagged.
7. Once inside a hospital, a dead ant can get back on their feet and return to the game.
8. Continue play for 1-2 minutes, or until the energy starts to fade.

Variations

- For really large groups (30+ people) introduce two or more ants and/or spread the ant hospitals further apart.
- Encourage ants to visit a designated 'picnic' area, periphery to the playing space, as often as possible to earn collective points for their ant colony. To earn a point, an ant must place any part of their body inside the designated area for two seconds (without being tagged.) Of course, they are recommended to save lost souls in the process.

Reflection

- What emotions did you experience as a Dead Ant?
- How often did you put yourself at risk to save one of your colleagues? Why?
- What risks do we take in our ordinary lives? Do we benefit from these decisions?

Basketball Court Tag

Structured tag game that directs your group's activity.

Benefits

- Simple
- Structured
- Promotes critical-thinking
- Multiple variations

People 8+

Time 2-5 mins

Instructions

1. Ask the members of your group to stand on most, if not all, of the painted lines of a basketball court.

2. One person volunteers as 'It,' ie their only goal is to tag someone.

3. On "GO" all movements – to tag or avoid being tagged – must occur on the lines.

4. A person can not jump from one line to another, or cut corners.

5. Once a tag has occurred, the role of 'It' immediately switches to newly-tagged person.

6. Continue play for several minutes, or try a variation while your group still has energy.

Variations

- Introduce two or more taggers, and watch the 'you-can't-get-away' strategies develop.
- Require that all movement (to tag and flee) reflect a particular type of physical movement, eg side-to-side, backwards, heel to toe, etc.

Reflection

- Was it challenging to limit your movements to the lines?
- Did you ever get cornered by 'It?' How did that feel?
- Were you ever tempted to jump lines, or cut a corner?

Name Tag

Challenging & highly-interactive name-based tag game.

Benefits

- Simple, but not easy
- Highly-interactive
- Name reminder
- Demands critical-thinking

People 8+

Time 5-10 mins

Instructions

1. Spread your group throughout a designated area.
2. Everyone has three 'lives' and their task is to avoid losing a life for as long as possible.
3. Everyone starts by walking around the area, no running.
4. As you are walking, randomly tag one person on their shoulder.
5. This tagged person must quickly call the name of another person (other than 'It.')
6. The named-person will become the new 'It' and immediately tag someone new.
7. This process will repeat itself – a tag is made, a name is called, a tag is made, a new name is called, etc.
8. A person may lose a 'life' in one of four ways:
   - Just-been-named did not tag a new person quickly;
   - Just-been-tagged did not call a name quickly;
   - Just-been-tagged called the name of their tagger (It) or an eliminated person; or
   - The tagger (It) calls out a name as they tag someone.
9. Once a person has lost three lives, they are eliminated from the game.
10. Continue playing until three final people remain, or the energy starts to wane.

Variations

- Vary the number of 'lives' a person may start with, ie everyone has one life.
- People lose a life if they "UMM," "ERR" or otherwise stall to call a new name.

Reflection

- How difficult was this game to play? Why?
- Did you apply any useful strategies to help you stay in the game?
- Where else in your life does 'multi-tasking' impair your performance?

CHAPTER 12

Trust-Building Exercises

Trust is a fragile thing and should be developed slowly and purposefully. While some degree of trust is involved in every program experience, a series of dedicated 'trust' exercises can provide an opportunity for the members of your group to commit their physical and emotional well-being at a higher level. These experiences are critical to the development and strengthening of relationships.

Trust-building games and exercises are safe and effective if they feature:

- Graduated series of activities in which risk-taking is encouraged
- Lots of physical and verbal interactions
- Support and co-operation of all group members
- Emphasis on Stretch Zone experiences
- 1 to 30 minutes of play

Partners

Spot The Difference – Come To Me – Hug A Tree – Human Camera – Pairs Compass Walk

Whole Group

Must Choose – This Or That – Look-Up Look-Down – Coming & Going Of The Rain
Funny Walk – Hog Call – Moon Walking – The Gauntlet – I Trust You, But...
Trust Wave – Slice & Dice

Spotting Skills Sequence

Palm Off – Trust Leans – Trust Line – Wind In The Willows – Levitation

Some activities in this chapter require significant & skilled support to attend to the physical & emotional wellbeing of your group.
To help keep your group safe, you are recommended to read & follow the safety guidelines of effective spotting skills (Part Three.)

Spot The Difference

Fun partner exercise to sharpen observation skills.

Benefits

- Simple
- Sharpens observation skills
- Inspires creativity
- Partner activity

People 2+

Time 5-10 mins

Instructions

1. Form pairs, standing back to back.

2. Instruct each person to change three things about their appearance within 30 seconds.

3. When time has expired, each person turns around to face their partner.

4. Taking turns, each person attempts to identify each of the three changes which their partner made.

5. Repeat, asking each person to make a further three changes to their appearance.

Variations

- Establish groups of four (or six) people, and invite two (or three) people to identify all of the changes in the other two (or three) people.

- Pairs remain back-to-back throughout the whole exercise. Their challenge is to recall or remember as many details about their partner as they can, such as colour of their clothing, which way they part their hair, shirt tucked in or not, etc. This exercise often highlights the little details we do not notice.

Reflection

- Was it difficult for you to change three (or six) things about your appearance?

- Where did you focus most of your attention to spot the difference in your partner?

- Early on, did you think to change your facial expressions, or attitude? Why?

Come To Me

Fun partner game that develops trust & listening skills.

Benefits

- Exciting
- Sharpens listening skills
- Develops trust
- Ideal for outdoors

People 2+

Time 10-15 mins

Instructions

1. Form pairs.
2. One partner moves approx 10 metres away (in full view) of their partner.
3. To start, the partner who did not move will close their eyes or put on a blindfold and call "COME TO ME."
4. The goal of the sighted person is to approach and tap the shoulder of their 'blind' partner within sixty seconds without being detected.
5. The 'blind' person is entitled to point five times in the direction of where they think their partner is lurking.
6. If the sighted person is successfully detected, or the 'blind' partner is tapped on their shoulder, the round is over.
7. Play several rounds, swapping roles each time.

Variations

- The sighted person's goal is to touch their partner as quickly as possible without detection.
- Blindfold multiple people, spread randomly throughout the area. Ask one sighted person to attempt to move from one side of the area to the other without being detected by any of the others. Each blindfolded person has a maximum of two guesses.

Reflection

- How did it feel to sneak up to someone who could not see you? Why?
- How did it feel to be the blindfolded person knowing someone was trying to sneak up to you?
- How easy was it to filter out all of the distractions and focus on your goal?

Hug A Tree

Gentle partner exercise that heightens the senses.

Benefits

- Passive
- Promotes communication
- Develops trust
- Partner activity

People 2+

Time 5-10 mins

Instructions

1. Form pairs.
2. Partners take it in turns to be blindfolded while the other leads them to a unique object approx 20-30 metres away.
3. The blindfolded person may spend up to 20 seconds becoming familiar with the shape, feel and smell of the object, before their partner returns them blindfolded back to where they started.
4. With their vision restored, the blindfolded person will then attempt to relocate the exact item they were introduced to.
5. Repeat this process at least twice, swapping roles between rounds.

Variations

- Form groups of three people, where two co-joined people are blindfolded at the same time. Tales of differing opinion often occur regarding distance, direction and the identification of the object.
- Introduce the blindfolded person to a set of similar items, eg stack of books, or garments of clothing. They are provided with just one item, and then upon returning it to the stack, the blindfolded person aims to relocate it.

Reflection

- What strategies did you use to remember and/or re-locate your object? Were they effective?
- What senses did you rely on the most?
- Did you discover anything about the object that surprised you?

Human Camera

Dynamic trust exercise to heighten observation skills.

Benefits

- Creative
- Attention to detail
- Fosters trust & support
- Partner activity

People 2+

Time 10-15 mins

Instructions

1. Form pairs.
2. Partners take it in turns to be blindfolded while the other leads them to a series of three random objects.
3. At each object, the sighted partner will describe the necessary focus, distance and exposure for their 'human camera' to capture an image (in their mind.)
4. On "GO" the 'blind' partner will open their eyes very briefly to capture a snapshot.
5. This process is repeated three times, before all pairs return to where they started.
6. The blindfolded people aim to remember three distinct images.
7. Re-gather your group, and invite a discussion about what each 'blind' person recorded in their mind's eye.
8. Repeat this process at least twice, swapping roles between rounds.

Variations

- Invite teams of pairs to view exactly the same objects with similar apertures, exposures and foci. Before switching roles, discuss what images each of the blindfolded people captured and compare.
- Train the lens of the blindfolded person to capture three images all taken in the same direction but focused on three different distances, eg 1, 10 and 50 metres away.

Reflection

- What surprised you about being a human camera?
- With practice, did you observation skills improve? Why?
- What might this exercise teach us about our observation skills?

Pairs Compass Walk

*Fun, trust-building navigation
exercise for partners.*

Benefits

- Sharpens senses
- Builds trust & empathy
- Fosters collaboration
- Partner activity

People 2+

Time 10-15 mins

Instructions

1. Form pairs.

2. One person identifies an object that is at least 50 metres away.

3. This person will then close their eyes, or put on a blindfold, and aim to walk in a straight line directly towards the object, stopping directly in front of it.

4. Meanwhile, the sighted person will walk silently behind their partner and prevent the latter from hitting any unforeseen obstacles.

5. Note the results of each attempt they make, observing accuracy, biases, etc.

6. Swap roles and repeat several times.

Variations

- Ask two people (possibly with opposite biases) to walk hand in hand. Their original partners will walk directly behind the two co-joined people to make observations, and ensure their safe progress.

- Take a look at **Group Compass Walk** to explore the group initiative form of this exercise.

Reflection

- What did you notice as the blind person travelling to your nominated destination?

- Which sense was more accurate for you - direction or distance?

- Did anything help or hinder your attempts to arrive at your destination?

Must Choose

Conversation starter that explores personal choices.

Benefits

- Simple set-up
- Fun get-to-know-you game
- Promotes communication
- Fosters critical-thinking

People 8+

Time 15-20 mins

Instructions

1. Form pairs.
2. Pose a question in which each person must choose between two distinct (often opposing) options, eg do you prefer Coke or Pepsi? Or, scan the QR code below to access dozens of sample questions as a subscriber.
3. Each person considers their choice and shares this decision with their partner.
4. Next, each person predicts the preference of the majority of people in their group, and shares this prediction with their partner.
5. When ready, ask everyone to stand to one side of a space (or the other) according to their personal choice to determine the majority preference of the group.
6. Each person who accurately predicts the group's (majority) preference earns a point.
7. Repeat this process, asking as many questions as you have time or energy to explore.

Variations

- Pose your question and ask each person to move to that side of the space which reflects their choice. Beware, this set-up may cause some people to be influenced by the decisions of others because there is no accountability built into each round.
- Take a look at **This Or That** for a similar conversation starter which explores the preference for one of two difficult-to-choose, hypothetical propositions.

Reflection

- How easy was it for you to make a decision?
- What factors or criteria did you use to make certain decisions?
- What might this game reveal about you and your group's values?

This Or That

Conversation starter that explores difficult propositions.

Benefits

- Simple set-up
- Deeper get-to-know-you game
- Promotes communication
- Fosters critical-thinking

People 8+

Time 15-20 mins

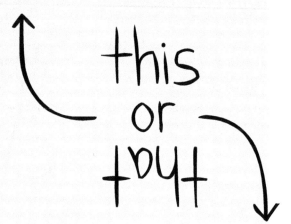

Instructions

1. Form pairs.
2. Pose a question in which each person must choose between two difficult, hypothetical propositions, eg would you prefer to be poor in a job you love, or rich in a job you hate? Or, scan the QR code below to access dozens of sample questions as a subscriber.
3. Each person considers their choice and shares this decision with their partner.
4. Next, each person predicts the preference of the majority of people in their group, and shares this prediction with their partner.
5. When ready, ask everyone to stand to one side of a space (or the other) according to their personal choice to determine the majority preference of the group.
6. Each person who accurately predicts the group's (majority) preference earns a point.
7. Repeat this process, asking as many questions as you have time or energy to explore.

Variations

- Simply pose your question and ask each person to move to that side of the space which reflects their choice, ie there is no sharing with a partner prior to the split.
- Take a look at **Must Choose** for a similar conversation starter which explores the preference for one of two, often opposing choices.

Reflection

- What factors or criteria did you use to make certain decisions?
- Did any of your choices surprise others who know you?
- What 'evidence' did you take into account to make your decisions?

Look-Up Look-Down

*Engaging, highly-interactive
& fun group energiser.*

Benefits

- Simple
- Energising
- Highly-interactive
- Promotes trust

People 8+

Time   1-2 mins

Instructions

1. Form a circle, asking your group to place their arms on their neighbour's shoulders.
2. When you say "LOOK UP" everyone looks straight up into the air.
3. When you say "LOOK DOWN" everyone casts their eyes down and directly at the eyes of one specific person in the circle.
4. When two people happen to look directly at each other, they immediately let out a scream and leave the circle.
5. The circle rejoins, and continues the looking up and down routine.
6. Those who leave the circle form a second circle, and restart the looking up and down process.
7. People move between the two circles with each round.
8. Continue play for 1 to 2 minutes.

Variations

- Start with two circles positioned far apart, and require pairs who depart one circle to run to the other. Brilliant for raising heart-rates.
- Use this game to generate random partners, ie comprising the two people who look at each other. Mutual pairs depart the circle, the circle rejoins and the pairing process continues until everyone has a partner.

Reflection

- How did it feel in this game to observe someone looking straight at you?
- Generally, how do you respond when you lock eyes with a stranger? Why?
- Why do you think it is so difficult to look someone, anyone, in the eye?

Coming & Going Of The Rain

Very soothing & entertaining large group energiser.

Benefits

- Simple & engaging
- Ideal for large groups
- Non-verbal communication
- Passive

People 12+

Time 1-2 mins

Instructions

1. In view of your group, start to rub your open palms together in front of you.
2. In response to your non-verbal urgings, invite your group to copy your moves.
3. Next, rub your hands more vigorously and then start to click your fingers.
4. Then use two fingers of one hand to clap into your opposite palm, before gradually morphing into full open-palmed clapping.
5. Crouch over and bending your knees, start to slap your palms onto your thighs.
6. Finally, while slapping your thighs vigorously, stamp one or both feet onto the floor or ground.
7. Once you have reached a crescendo, slowly reverse the motions until you are slowly rubbing your hands together again.

Variations

- Introduce a variety of sounds from tongue-clicks, whistles, thigh-slaps, hoots and hollering! Just make it fun.
- Ask your group to stand and form a tight circle, with each person facing the back of the person in front of them. With eyes closed, ask each person to mirror the identical stroke (they receive from the person behind them) onto the back of the person in front of them. As leader, start with slow, gentle strokes, and gradually build up the pace and intensity of the beats in an attempt to mimic the sound of a passing rain storm.

Reflection

- What did you first think when the activity started?
- What feelings did you experience as the activity progressed? Good, bad, other?
- What was the impact of this exercise on the group when the rain passed?

Funny Walk

Fun & dynamic group initiative to build trust & empathy.

Benefits

- Playful & fun
- Develops trust
- Promotes collaboration
- Inspires creativity

People 8+

Time   10-15 mins

Instructions

1. Assemble group at one end of a wide open space, possibly behind a line.

2. Every person is invited to walk from one side of the space to the other in the most inventive, zany manner they can think of.

3. When the group arrives at the other end, form pairs and repeat the crossing, without repeating any walking styles that have already been used.

4. All crossings must involve some form of physical contact between partners.

5. Next crossing, two pairs form into groups of four.

6. Then, two groups of four form into groups of eight people, and so on.

7. People cross back and forth, until the final crossing involves the whole group.

Variations

- Adopt this silliness to move a group a long distance, progressing forward about 10 to 20 metres (30 - 60') with each round, until you arrive at your destination.

- Remain in small groups of 2 to 4 people, and challenge them to invent as many unique methods to 'walk' from one side of the space to the other.

Reflection

- How did you feel as you walked on the first crossing? Why?
- Was it easy or difficult to invent progressively new ways to walk?
- What do you think was the primary objective for an exercise like this?

Hog Call

Fun trust-building exercise with a focus on communication.

Benefits

- Playful & fun
- Promotes trust
- Develops communication skills
- Multiple variations

People 8+

Time 5-10 mins

Instructions

1. Form pairs.
2. Each pair identifies a favourite animal, and the sound associated with it, eg a cow and moo.
3. Invite each pair to announce their animal and express its sound (to avoid duplication.)
4. Pairs split, with each person moving to the opposite end of a designated playing space to their partner.
5. Getting ready, each person turns away from their partner, shuffles their position, closes their eyes and assumes the bumpers up position.
6. On "GO" each person turns and walks towards their partner (blind) and starts calling their animal's noise in an effort to find one another.
7. As each pair reunites, they may open their eyes.

Variations

- Each pair identifies a set of two words which are associated, such as salt + pepper, coca + cola and peanut + butter. Name each person after one of the words. Only this word is called by their partner in an effort to locate them in the blind confusion.
- Use words that are significant and/or relevant to your group, such as positive attributes of the organisation, or strengths of the team, etc. In this case, partners will share the same word.

Reflection

- How easy was it to hear your partner's calls? Why?
- How did it feel to locate your partner?
- What might this exercise teach us about communicating effectively?

Moon Walking

Extremely fun & dynamic energiser that builds trust.

Benefits

- Exciting challenge
- Physically active
- Promotes collaboration
- Builds trust & empathy

People 2+

Time 5-10 mins

Instructions

1. Assemble your group within a wide, open space.

2. Form into teams of three people.

3. By way of demonstration, ask one person to place their hands firmly on their hips, while their two partners grab a lower arm each with their two hands.

4. When ready, ask the middle person to jump high into the air from a standing start, while their partners gently assist their lift into the air.

5. Emphasise that this extra support must be dispensed gently, firmly and continuously.

6. Allow time for each person to experience being the jumper.

7. Swaps partners and repeat, or try a variation.

Variation

- After a series of preparatory on-site jumps, invite the threesome to move forward five paces, stepping forward in rapid succession with each jump. It will feel almost like they are flying.

Reflection

- How high could you jump without assistance?

- What did it feel like to jump a lot higher with help?

- Name at least three different ways you received or gave support. How did you benefit?

The Gauntlet

Ideal trust-building & spotting skills practice exercise.

Benefits

- Tactile
- Develops safety consciousness
- Sharpens observation skills
- Promotes critical-thinking

People 12+

Time 2-5 mins

Instructions

1. Form two lines, standing shoulder to shoulder, facing each other about 1.5 metres apart.

2. Stand at the opening of one end of the two lines, facing your group.

3. Group assumes the agreed 'spotting' position (refer Chapter 15 for guidance.)

4. Upon issuing a series of agreed 'Are-you-ready?' commands, walk slowly between the two lines.

5. Adopting an unsteady manner, attempt to walk to the end of the two lines, falling randomly at any time.

6. Group aims to protect you from falling to the ground, and when you do, returns you to equilibrium, each time.

7. Repeat with several volunteers.

Variations

- With young people, suggest that they are very tired and wonky on their feet, and for adults, they are walking home from the pub after a big night of drinking! Observe the fun index sky-rocket.

- Do it blindfolded (the walker, not the spotters.)

Reflection

- What did you notice as you walked through the two lines of spotters?
- What did you notice as a spotter?
- Which role felt like it was the most vulnerable? Why?

I Trust You, But...

Very dynamic trust-building & spotting skills exercise.

Benefits

- Tactile
- Entertaining
- Sharpens observation skills
- Promotes critical-thinking

People 8+

Time 15-20 mins

Instructions

1. Ask a volunteer to move at least 25 metres away from the rest of the group.
2. Rest of your group forms a line of 'spotters' facing the volunteer, side-by-side about arm's length apart (refer Chapter 15 for guidance.)
3. Upon issuing a series of agreed 'Are-you-ready?' commands, ask the volunteer to close their eyes, place their hands in front of their face, and run at three-quarter pace directly towards the line of spotters.
4. Runner should aim to maintain a constant pace and only stop when the spotters make contact with their hands.
5. Spotters aim to stop the runner from passing through their line, by meeting the runner's hands with their own.
6. Repeat with several volunteers.

Variations

- Runners are instructed to stop running just short of the end. This is bound to spark a lot of amusement as many people discover just how poor their sense of direction and distance is.
- Invite two people, holding hands (still with eyes closed) to be runners at the same time. Note the interplay between the couple as one reacts differently to the other, and the impact this has on the other.

Reflection

- As spotters, what did you notice as the runner approached you? What did you make this mean?
- As a runner, what did you think or feel as you approached the spotters?
- Why do you think the runners often slowed down towards the end? Is this a reasonable reaction?

Trust Wave

Exciting trust-building experience that sharpens reflexes.

Benefits

- Exciting
- Playful & fun
- Promotes collaboration
- Develops trust

People 12+

Time 10-15 mins

Instructions

1. Form two straight lines of people, facing each other, standing about 1-2 metres apart.
2. Instruct these people to extend their arms out in front of them (parallel to the ground) alternating their arms between the people opposite.
3. Ask a volunteer to stand at least 10 metres from one of the ends of the two lines, looking straight down the middle.
4. Upon issuing a series of agreed 'Are-you-ready?' commands, ask the volunteer to run at three-quarter pace directly towards the corridor between the two lines.
5. The two lines of people aim to keep their arms out-stretched until the very last moment the runner passes in front of them, when they rapidly flick their arms up out of the way.
6. Runner is challenged to maintain an even pace through the corridor and out the end of the two lines before stopping, keeping their eyes open at all times.
7. Aim to create an exciting thrill for the runner while not hitting him or her in the process.
8. Repeat with several volunteers.

Variations

- Move the two lines of people further away from each other, so that their hands or arms do not overlap. Indeed, you could add a gap between the fingertips of each line, all in an effort to reduce the perceived risk.
- Take a look at **Slice & Dice** as an ideal exercise to progress from the Trust Wave.

Reflection

- What did you observe as the runner approached the two lines of arms? What did you make this mean?
- Did the runner maintain a consistent pace? Why or why not?
- How did it feel to be the runner? Did you trust the group would react in time?

Slice & Dice

Exhilarating trust-building game that pushes boundaries.

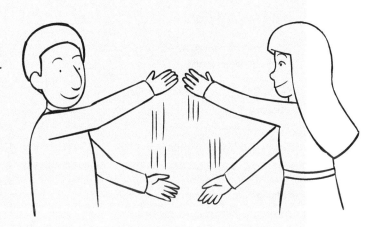

Benefits

- Exciting
- Playful & fun
- Promotes collaboration
- Develops critical-thinking

People 12+

Time 10-15 mins

Instructions

1. Form two straight lines of people, facing each other, standing 1.5 to 2 metres apart.
2. Instruct these people to swing their arms full stretch in front of them up and down in a chopping motion.
3. Ask a volunteer to stand at least 2 metres from one of the ends of the two lines, looking straight down the middle.
4. Upon issuing a series of agreed 'Are-you-ready?' commands, ask the volunteer to walk down the corridor between the two lines.
5. The two lines of people aim to slice the air with their swinging arms and hands directly in front of the walker as he or she passes by.
6. The walker aims to maintain an even pace down the corridor until they exit the two lines, keeping their eyes open at all times.
7. Aim to create an exciting thrill for the walker, while not hitting them in the process.
8. Repeat with several volunteers.

Variations

- Move the two lines of people further away from each other, so that their hands or arms do not overlap, ie to reduce the perceived risk for the walker.
- For truly advanced and switched-on groups, invite the volunteer to jog through the lines at the recommended three-quarter pace.

Reflection

- What did you observe as the walker passed by? What did you make this mean?
- How did it feel to be the walker?
- Did you trust the group would attend to your safety? How and why?

Palm Off

Quick partner energiser to teach principles of balance.

Benefits

- Playful & fun
- Quick & simple
- Promotes critical-thinking
- Partner activity

People 2+

Time 1-2 mins

Instructions

1. Form pairs, facing one another with feet together and toes about half-metre apart.

2. To start, each person raises their hands, palms facing forward towards their partner.

3. Each person aims to knock their partner off-balance, ie their feet move back or forward to regain balance.

4. The only contact an individual may make with their partner is palm to palm.

5. After several short rounds, swap partners.

Variations

- To ramp up the challenge, reduce the distance between the toes of the two partners, so that they are almost touching.

- Invite each partner to squat down, balancing on the balls of their feet to play. Each person attempts to cause the other to fall forward onto their hands or backwards onto their heels to win.

Reflection

- Would you describe this game as fun? Why?
- Was it easy to lose your balance? Why?
- What might this game teach us about effective spotting skills?

Trust Leans

Fun exercise to develop trust, support & spotting skills.

Benefits

- Exciting
- Promotes trust & empathy
- Develops critical-thinking
- Partner activity

People 2+

Time 5-10 mins

Instructions

1. Form pairs.
2. One person (faller) stands with feet together, with their back to their partner (spotter.)
3. The faller stands firm and places their arms across their chest.
4. The spotter positions themselves with one foot in front of the other, hands-up in 'ready' position behind the faller.
5. Upon issuing a series of agreed 'Are-you-ready?' commands, the faller leans back slowly into the hands of the spotter a small distance.
6. Upon being supported, the spotter returns the faller to the standing position.
7. Repeat these steps several times, allowing the faller to fall back a little further with each attempt, as far as each person is comfortable.
8. Swap roles, and then swap partners.

Variations

- Invite the faller to lean forward towards their spotter. The skills required to spot the front of a person are similar to their back, but the forward spotter is advised to use the faller's crossed upper-arms to catch their lean, ie to avoid embarrassing hands-on-chest issues.
- Start with three people, two spotters each facing a third person – the faller – standing between them. This time, the faller may lean backwards or forwards, and at any time. Generally, as the spotters support each lean, they return the faller to the centre and this momentum causes them to develop a gentle rocking, back-and-forth motion.

Reflection

- What emotions came up for you during this experience?
- How did it feel to lean back and trust your partner? Did you commit fully?
- What might this exercise teach us about developing significant relationships?

Trust Line

Powerful trust-building exercise for small groups.

Benefits

- Powerful Trust Leans variation
- Builds trust & empathy
- Promotes collaboration
- Develops critical-thinking

People 8+

Time 15-20 mins

Instructions

1. Form one straight line, with one half of the group facing the other half of the group.

2. Invite a volunteer (the faller) to stand between the two people facing each other in the middle of the line.

3. The two people directly facing the 'faller' will assume a spotter's stance, ie one foot forward, hands up, eyes straight ahead.

4. The volunteer assumes a comfortable 'faller' position, ie arms crossed on chest, feet together, body firm.

5. Upon issuing a series of 'Are you ready?' calls, the faller will choose to lean forwards or backwards into the waiting arms of one of the two spotters.

6. This spotter will absorb the weight of the faller, and then gently return them to their starting position.

7. With a little momentum, this gentle push will allow the faller to lean gently into the arms of the other spotter.

8. After each spotter has returned the faller to their starting position, they will immediately step out of the line to their left and join the end of the line they were facing.

9. Immediately, the next person in line steps forward and prepares to 'spot' the faller when they next lean towards their direction.

10. The faller aims to rock back and forth many times, supported by a series of new individual spotters with each lean.

11. Spotters constantly change their position relative to the faller, as much as the line in which they are standing.

12. Allow this gentle rocking process to continue for 15 to 30 seconds, then stop.

13. Invite a new volunteer to become the next faller.

14. Continue until everyone has been given the opportunity to be a faller.

Variations

- Invite any individual spotter to remain in an active spotting position, supporting the weight of the faller several times, before stepping out of the line. Naturally, the randomness of this routine heightens the need for the next-in-line to be ready at any moment's notice.

- Take a look at **Palm Off**, **Trust Leans**, **The Gauntlet** and **Wind in the Willows** to augment your efforts to present a series of useful preparatory experiences.

Reflection

- As a faller, what helped you feel comfortable or uncomfortable?

- As a spotter, what did you observe or feel?

- What skills do you think this exercise developed within the group?

Refer to Chapter 15 to review useful spotting skills guidelines.

Wind In The Willows

Powerful trust-building exercise to support small groups.

Benefits

- Exciting
- Promotes trust & empathy
- Develops support skills
- Fosters collaboration

People 8+

Time 20-30 mins

Instructions

1. Form a group of 8 to 12 people, and stand in a circle.
2. Invite one person (the faller) to stand in the middle of the circle, with their feet together and arms crossed on their chest.
3. The spotters position themselves with one foot in front of the other, hands-up in ready position close to the faller (refer to Chapter 15 for guidance.)
4. Upon issuing a series of agreed 'Are you ready?' commands, the faller will lean or fall in any direction they choose.
5. Initially, ask the group to support the weight of the faller all the way around the circle.
6. Continue passing the faller in any direction, gradually increasing the distance of the falls and passes, for 15 to 30 seconds.
7. Repeat these steps with as many volunteers who wish to participate as the faller.

Variations

- Upon completing the typical back and forth motions, transition the faller into a position so that you can morph into **Levitation**.
- Invite the circle of spotters to sit down using their feet and legs to form a tight circle around the feet of the faller. This position effectively locks the faller's feet into position while the spotters raise their arms above their heads to support the falls. Note – this option is significantly more dynamic, and should only be presented to highly-competent spotters.

Reflection

- As a faller, what helped you feel comfortable or uncomfortable?
- As a spotter, did your role differ from other trust-building activities?
- What did you learn that helps us understand how to look after one another?

Levitation

Powerful & enjoyable trust-building activity for groups.

Benefits

- Exciting
- Promotes trust & empathy
- Fosters collaboration
- Develops support skills

People 8

Time 15-20 mins

Instructions

1. Ask for a volunteer to stand in the middle of a group of at least eight people.
2. Volunteer will place their feet together, cross their arms on their chest and keep their body stiff.
3. Upon issuing a series of agreed 'Are you ready?' commands, the group leans the volunteer backwards, until their head and upper torso are supported.
4. Lifting together, the group then slowly elevates the volunteer's body off the ground to shoulder height.
5. Once comfortable, the group then starts rocking the person's body back and forth (from head to toe) several times.
6. After about 15 to 20 seconds, the group lowers the person gently to the ground.
7. Repeat these steps with as many volunteers who wish to participate.

Variations

- Once elevated, instruct the group to silently (and secretly) carry the levitating person to a non-disclosed location, all the while rocking them on their journey. Choose to do this randomly to keep the levitating person guessing.
- Transition from the conclusion of **Wind In The Willows** to a levitation. Use a silent gesture to halt the group's passing motions, lean the 'faller' backwards so that their head and neck can be supported, and then prepare for a lift.

Reflection

- What was your most significant part of the levitation experience?
- What were you aware of during the levitation?
- What helped you to feel comfortable (or uncomfortable) during the exercise?

CHAPTER 13

Group Problem-Solving Initiatives

This chapter features many wonderful group experiences which invite your group to solve a problem that often has more than one 'answer.' They are ideal for developing critical interpersonal skills such as communication, collaboration, critical-thinking and creativity.

Problem-solving and team-building exercises often stimulate significant growth for a group, especially when group members are invited to reflect on what they have learned during the activity.

- Group initiatives typically feature the following characteristics:
- Physical and verbal interaction among group members
- High levels of arousal, challenge and excitement
- Opportunities for trust, leadership, communication and collaboration to evolve
- Focus on the process, not just the task
- 2 to 30 minutes of play

Low Exertion

Name Train – Mute Line-Up – Quick Shuffle – About Now – Sherpa Walk
Circle Clap – Izzat You? – Group Compass Walk – Body English – Negotiation

High Exertion

Four Up – Don't Touch Me – Span The Room – Human Knot – Lap Circle
Magic Shoes – Everybody Up – Popsicle Push-Up – The Clock – Four Pointer

Name Train

Introductory group initiative that creates random pairs.

Benefits

- Simple
- Promotes collaboration
- Fosters critical-thinking
- Creates random pairs

People 12+

Time 2-5 mins

nate   eliza   aaron   nora

Instructions

1. Each person notes the first and last letters of their first name, eg J and A if your name was Jessica.

2. Group aims to pair every person with one other person who shares one of these two letters.

3. Challenge your group to continue to mix and match partners until everyone is successfully paired.

4. If necessary, continue to seek a solution until the group agrees it can not be found.

Variations

- For small groups (say, less than 10 people) or for groups which include names featuring less-common letters (eg Q and X) involve the first and last letters of both the first and last names of each person. If success still eludes your group, permit the first and last letters of all first, middle and last names.

- Challenge your group to form one straight line (or even a circle, if at all possible) whereby every person is linked by the first or last letter of their left and right neighbours.

Reflection

- Was this task challenging? Why or why not?
- What was necessary to help the group achieve success?
- As soon as you paired with another person, what happened to your focus?

Mute Line-Up

Simple initiative with focus on effective communication.

Benefits

- Introductory challenge
- Develops communication
- Inspires creativity
- Promotes collaboration

People 8+

Time 5-10 mins

Instructions

1. Gather your group and tell them that they are mute, no talking from this point forward.
2. Challenge them to form one straight line according to a set criteria, eg date and month of their birth.
3. Only non-verbal forms of communication can be used at any time.
4. Once the line is formed, check the accuracy of the sequence.

Variations

- Ask your group to wear blindfolds (and not talk) to limit another useful faculty.
- Here is a non-exhaustive list of some popular line-up criteria - shoe size, date of birth (not including the year,) date of a particular event or memory, street address number, zip or postcode, last two digits of home telephone or mobile number, middle name (alphabetical order,) year of manufacture of coin randomly passed out, number of years employed, schooled, married, etc, favourite animal (alphabetical based on charade,) size or length of random object just picked up (eg a stick,) number of letters in full name (first, middle, last.)

Reflection

- What did you notice as the activity progressed?
- What was the most challenging part of the exercise? Why?
- What principles of effective communication are featured in this activity?

Quick Shuffle

Introductory problem-solving exercise for small groups.

Benefits

- Passive challenge
- Sharpens observation skills
- Fosters collaboration
- Promotes communication

People 8+

Time   15-20 mins

Instructions

1. Seven people stand in one line, side-by-side, facing the rest of the group.
2. Observe these seven people for ten seconds.
3. Instruct the 'looking' group to close their eyes.
4. Ask the seven people to shuffle their positions.
5. Upon re-opening their eyes, challenge the 'looking' group to re-shuffle the seven people back to their original positions.
6. Swap roles, and repeat several times.

Variations

- For large groups, create several sets of seven, with matching groups of two or three people to do the looking and re-shuffling.
- Moving only one person at a time, record how many moves it takes for the looking group to correctly re-shuffle the line.

Reflection

- What did you notice about your looking group's process in the beginning?
- Did you encounter disagreements? Did you reach a resolution? How?
- What strategies did your looking group use to re-shuffle more successfully in later rounds?

About Now

Simple problem-solving exercise for small & large groups.

Benefits

- Simple set-up
- Develops critical-thinking
- Inspires creativity
- Tests perception skills

People 8+

Time 10-15 mins

Instructions

1. In advance, lay or mark two 'lines' spaced about 10 to 20 metres apart.
2. Assemble your group to stand behind one of these lines, facing the other line.
3. When ready, each person aims to cross the farthest line when they think exactly 60 seconds has elapsed.
4. No talking is permitted at any time.
5. Mentally note the people who cross the line closest to the one minute mark.
6. Repeat the task several times to measure overall group improvement.
7. Allow time for planning and problem-solving discussions between rounds.

Variations

- Allow group members to communicate with each other before and during the exercise, with the objective of having everyone crossing the line at the same time. Aim for group consensus where everyone makes one simultaneous step as close to one minute as possible.
- Start your group by standing, and instructing individuals to sit down exactly as 60 seconds expires.

Reflection

- In general, did 60 seconds pass quicker or slower than you estimated?
- As a group, how well did we estimate the passing of 60 seconds?
- How much of the 'flurry' of most of you stepping over the line at about the same time suggests that we are easily influenced by others? Why?

Sherpa Walk

Fun blindfold exercise to sharpen communication skills.

Benefits

- Playful & fun
- Promotes trust & empathy
- Promotes communication
- Ideal transition exercise

People 8+

Time 10-15 mins

Instructions

1. In teams of 8 to 12 people, form a straight line facing the back of the person in front.
2. Each person holds the hand of the person in front of them and closes their eyes.
3. Nominate yourself as the 'sherpa.'
4. Holding the hand of the person at the front of the line, announce that you will now lead the group on a mystery journey.
5. Everyone must keep their eyes closed and remain physically connected to the group.
6. Encourage people to talk, especially to describe obstacles as they are encountered.
7. Guide the group on walk for up to 5 minutes, traversing a variety of obstacles, eg steps up or down, furniture, low-hanging branches, etc.
8. The group aims to arrive safely at the secret destination.
9. Once arrived, invite your group to reflect and discuss what they experienced on the walk.

Variations

- Lead your blindfolded group members only by verbal commands, that is, offer no physical assistance at all.
- Form pairs. Invite one person to be blindfolded at a time. The sighted person leads their partner verbally (not physically) on a journey from A to B via a series of obstacles/challenges.

Reflection

- Was your group successful? How do you define success?
- What strategies did your group use to communicate the passing of obstacles? Were they effective?
- How did you support one another throughout the exercise?

Circle Clap

Simple group initiative to teach synergy & collaboration.

Benefits

- Promotes collaboration
- Inspires creativity
- Focus on precision & goal-setting
- Fosters communication

People 8+

Time   5-10 mins

Instructions

1. Form a circle.
2. Ask group to work together to make the sound of one simultaneous clap.
3. No one can clap their own hands together, ie each person must involve their neighbour's hands to form a clap.
4. Allow time for discussion to solve the problem, or limit the number of attempts.

Variations

- Allow each person to create one simultaneous clapping sensation by using their own hands.
- Once you have achieved the single clap (either method) shoot for two (or more) single claps in a row, ie CLAP CLAP!

Reflection

- What did it take to achieve one simultaneous clap from the group?
- What were your biggest challenges? How did you solve these problems?
- Was it necessary for everyone to follow the same instructions?

Izzat You?

Blindfold group initiative to sharpen listening skills.

Benefits
- Playful & fun
- Dynamic
- Focus on effective communication
- Promotes collaboration

People 12+

Time 10-15 mins

Instructions

1. Form a circle.
2. Everyone turns to the person on their left and says 'HOW'S IT GOING?"
3. Then, everyone turns to the person on their right and says "IZZAT YOU?"
4. Repeat these greetings several times to respective neighbours.
5. When ready, close eyes, assume the Bumper's Up position and mix/mingle with others.
6. After 10 to 15 seconds, call "STOP" and remind everyone to keep their eyes closed.
7. Group is challenged to re-form the circle so that they are standing between their two original neighbours, saying only "HOW'S IT GOING?" and "IZZAT YOU?" to guide them.
8. Nothing else can be said or communicated at any time.
9. Aim to re-form the circle as accurately and as effectively as possible.
10. When it appears that the group has accomplished the task, they may open their eyes.

Variations

- Perform the task two or more times, inviting the group to develop strategies for reducing their time between rounds.
- Play **King Frog** at some point prior to this activity. When the group is appropriately mixed-up with their eyes closed, challenge your group to find their way back home by only making the noise of the very first animal they created.

Reflection

- What did you observe as everyone started to locate their neighbours?
- What helped you find your neighbours in the circle? What didn't help?
- As your sight was impaired, what other senses were used to assist you?

Group Compass Walk

Fun, trust-building navigation exercise for small groups.

Benefits

- Challenging
- Sharpens senses
- Builds trust & empathy
- Fosters collaboration

People 8+

Time 15-20 mins

Instructions

1. Position your group at one end or edge of a wide open space.
2. Nominate an object at the opposite end of the space, 50 to 100 metres away, eg a tree.
3. Group aims to walk in a straight line to this object with their eyes closed, stopping just short of the object.
4. Group must remain in total physical contact with one another at all times.
5. Group may stop and start as often they choose along their journey, and may communicate (with eyes closed) at all times.
6. Upon reaching its target, ask your group to keep their eyes closed and, as individuals, point in the direction of where they personally believe the object is situated.
7. Finally, ask everyone to open their eyes.
8. Invite your group to reflect on the outcome, and the process they undertook to plan and execute their journey.

Variations

- Silently drop an easy-to-see-at-a-distance item directly behind the group to mark their path. When you ask your group to look back, the line of items will invariably spark many oohs and ahhhs, not to mention a real sense of what was happening when. Even better, secretly perform this Hansel & Gretel flourish and delight in their surprise at the end.
- Take a look at **Pairs Compass Walk** for a similar trust-building exercise for pairs.

Reflection

- What observations did you make as your group travelled towards its target?
- Did your group progress as planned, or did you have to adjust along the way?
- Did your final destination surprise you? Why?

Body English

Simple communication exercise to foster creativity.

Benefits

- Playful & fun
- Promotes collaboration
- Develops critical-thinking
- Focus on effective communication

People 8+

Time 10-15 mins

Instructions

1. Create an even number of smaller groups, of approx 5 to 10 people.

2. Pair each small group to another, and ask one team (of each pair) to move about 50 metres away from the other.

3. Each 'sending' team aims to communicate a unique message to the 'receiving' team using their bodies to form the shape of letters of the alphabet.

4. The message will instruct the receiving team to do something, eg 'stand on one leg while singing a song.'

5. No verbal communication is permitted between groups at any time.

6. Teams are challenged to communicate the message, and then perform the action, as accurately and as quickly as possible.

Variations

- Devise a series of messages that feature alphabetic and numeric characters. Throw in a few punctuation marks for good fun too!

- Each group is challenged to 'relay' as many four or five-letter words as they can create in, say, four minutes.

Reflection

- What challenges did you encounter sending or receiving messages? How did you resolve these issues?

- Were there times when you were misunderstood? How did you respond?

- How might this exercise mirror communication in the 'real' world?

Negotiation

Extremely dynamic exercise which explores group consensus.

Benefits

- Focus on consensus & goal-setting
- Very dynamic
- Promotes collaboration
- Strong metaphors

People 4+

Time 20-30 mins

Instructions

1. Form three or four roughly even teams.
2. Each small team will move to a separate space to discuss and agree on a common non-verbal, physical gesture which reflects a prescribed theme, eg community.
3. After a few minutes, each team returns to the common space.
4. When ready, each team performs their gestures simultaneously, for approx 5 to 10 seconds, while observing the gestures of all other groups.
5. This concludes the first round.
6. Announce the ultimate goal is for all teams to achieve consensus in as few rounds as possible, whereby every team eventually performs an identical gesture.
7. No communication is permitted between teams at any time between or during the rounds.
8. Allow several minutes for discussion in small teams (in secluded areas) between rounds.
9. Conclude the activity after 8 rounds or when all teams have adopted the same gesture.

Variations

- Announce that the gestures must reflect something related or meaningful to your group or program goals, eg teamwork, community, world peace or some other nebulous theme.
- At the end of round three, permit one representative from each small team to meet in a neutral spot for 2 minutes to discuss anything they choose. Typically, the discussion will fall somewhere between 'do-it-our-way-because-it's-better' and 'let's-work-together.' Note, agreement among these folks does not necessarily beat a path to consensus.

Reflection

- Was it easy to let go of something important to you, and change? Why?
- Was consensus achieved? Why or why not?
- What did it take, or would it take, for one or more teams to change?

Four Up

Very fun, yet challenging group problem-solving activity.

Benefits

- Playful & fun
- Challenging
- Sharpens observation skills
- Promotes critical-thinking

People 12+

Time 5-10 mins

Instructions

1. Sit your group on the floor, or in chairs.
2. Announce that anyone is invited to stand whenever he or she wants to.
3. A person can not remain standing for longer than five seconds before they must sit down again.
4. Aim to have exactly four people standing at any point in time for as long as possible.
5. Play several rounds to record the longest time.

Variations

- Invite people to shoot a single hand (arm) into the air and down again. This version is less-active than its stand-up-sit-down cousin, and equally as challenging.
- Allow any four, five or six members of the group to be standing at any point in time. At first glance, this may seem a simpler task, but not always.

Reflection

- What did it take to be successful at this game?
- Was there a turning point in the exercise? Exactly when and why?
- What do you think was the purpose of this game?

Don't Touch Me

Fun group initiative that teaches value of collaboration.

Benefits

- Fosters teamwork
- Focus on continuous improvement
- Promotes communication
- Inspires creativity

People 8+

Time   20-30 mins

Instructions

1. Form two even teams.
2. Position the members of each team to stand on one of two opposing lines, eg sports-court lines, approximately 6 to 8 metres apart.
3. Mark a small circle (approx 1 metre diameter) exactly in the centre of the two teams.
4. Working together, the members of each team aim to switch sides, after passing through the small circle, as fast as possible.
5. To record an official attempt, there can be no physical contact between any team members at any time.
6. Allow at least three official attempts to record the fastest time.

Variations

- Require that each team re-position themselves (on the opposing line) in the same order as the line they started from.
- Start your group standing on a large circle, with a smaller circle directly in the centre. Each person is entitled to move to any spot in the circle (after passing through the smaller circle) that is not within 1 to 2 metres of their starting spot.

Reflection

- What was effective about your group's process to solve this problem? What wasn't?
- Did you group take any 'risks?' What were they? Were they worth it?
- What was necessary to help your group continuously improve?

Span The Room

*Challenging group initiative
that inspires creativity.*

Benefits

- Promotes ingenuity
- Fosters collaboration
- Develops critical-thinking
- Suits all abilities

People 4+

Time 20-30 mins

Instructions

1. Locate a wide area between two points, such as two opposing walls, two trees, etc.

2. Instruct your group to physically span the space between these two points using their bodies, forming a continuous connection between all people and the two ends.

3. To record an official attempt, the connection must be established for five seconds.

4. Over several consecutive rounds, challenge your group by progressively limiting the number and type of body parts which may touch the ground between the two points, eg five feet, two hands and one bottom.

5. Continue until your group is ultimately challenged.

Variations

- Challenge your group to use as many different parts of their collective anatomical parts (which touch the ground) to span between two points, eg score a point for each different body part that is used.

- Identify two opposing ends, and challenge your group to span the room between them with as few parts of the group's anatomy touching the ground.

Reflection

- Were you ever surprised by what was possible in this exercise? Why?
- What helped inspire and generate creative ideas? Provide examples.
- How many ideas were generated? Did you try them all? Why or why not?

Human Knot

Classic small group initiative with multiple variations.

Benefits

- Simple set-up
- Promotes communication
- Develops critical-thinking
- Demands focus & patience

People 8+

Time 20-30 mins

Instructions

1. Form a tight circle with everyone facing into the centre.

2. Instruct each person to extend one of their arms in front of themselves and then grab the hand of another person opposite them in the circle.

3. Repeat this process with the other arm, grabbing the hand of a different person.

4. When ready, group members aim to untangle themselves, without ever letting go of their partner's hands.

5. Continue to free as many people from the tangle until one or more circles are produced, or until the group agrees it can not proceed any further.

Variations

- If necessary, entitle the group to identify just one set of linked-hands that can be temporarily released and re-connected in a new position (of the group's choosing.) If pushed, you may apply this trick twice.

- Invite people to grab the ends of a short piece of rope, rather than a person's hand. Ideal for larger groups, and is a useful technique when close proximity for long periods could be an issue.

Reflection

- What skills were necessary to help your group be effective in this activity?
- How would you describe your communication and problem-solving processes?
- Were you successful? How do you define your success?

Lap Circle

*Fun group initiative to leverage
trust & collaboration.*

Benefits

- Quick
- Fun & engaging
- Promotes collaboration
- Circle game

People 8+

Time 2-5 mins

Instructions

1. Form a very tight circle, with each person facing to their left.

2. Each person places their hands gently onto the shoulders of the person in front of them.

3. Check that your group is actually standing in a circle, ie no corners.

4. When ready, invite everyone to slowly bend at their knees, push their butt out to gently sit down onto the lap of the person behind them.

5. Sit for as long as your group is comfortable.

Variations

- When settled, challenge your group to move their feet forward in unison, one foot at a time. Aim to rotate a full 360 degrees around the circle without falling to the ground. If this is too easy, walk backwards.

- Challenge your group to move laterally towards an object 5 to 10 metres away.

Reflection

- How did you feel as the group started to sit-down?
- What helped the effort to support one another? What didn't work?
- What did the group need to focus on, in particular, to be successful?

Magic Shoes

Physical group exercise that demands creativity & planning.

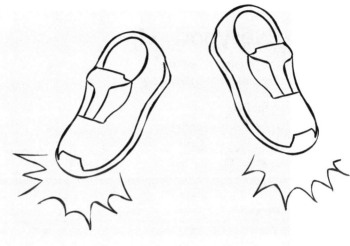

Benefits

- Physical & mental challenge
- Develops critical-thinking
- Promotes collaboration
- Focus on effective planning

People 8+

Time   20-30 mins

Instructions

1. Identify two 'safe' areas on the ground approx 10 metres apart.
2. Direct your group to stand in one of the two safe areas.
3. Your group's goal is to move every person to the other safe area without touching the hazardous pit in between.
4. To assist the group in their task, they will be given an imaginary pair of 'magic shoes' which, when worn, allow the wearer to cross the pit.
5. The magic shoes can only be worn by each person once, and then only in one direction.
6. Allow ample planning time, and then permit the group to make their first attempts to cross the pit.
7. Impose a time limit, or allow as many attempts as necessary to complete the task.

Variation

- Assuming one person can only ever carry one other person (at most) across the pit, challenge your group to calculate how many pairs of 'magic shoes' (blessed with powers as described above) would be required to move everyone to safety?

Reflection

- At what point did your group get stuck in its process? Why?
- What particular skills were critical to the success of this exercise?
- Did you feel that your role was important? Why?

Everybody Up

*Progressively challenging &
creative team-building exercise.*

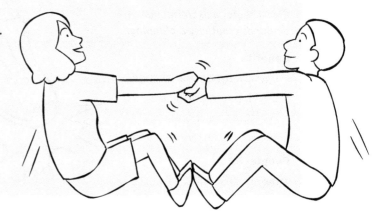

Benefits

- Fosters collaboration
- Inspires creativity
- Physically-demanding
- All group sizes

People 8+

Time 15-20 mins

Instructions

1. Form into pairs, preferably with someone of the same size.
2. Each pair sits facing one another, the balls of their feet touching, knees bent and hands tightly grasping their partner in front of them.
3. From this seated position, invite each pair to simultaneously lift themselves into an upright standing position.
4. Next, ask two successful pairs to join hands and attempt the same task as a group of four people.
5. Then challenge two groups of four people to become a group of eight people, etc.
6. Finally, the whole group connects with one another, and attempts to lift themselves off the ground simultaneously.

Variation

- Pairs start sitting back to back with their partner. With each success, add a further twosome, etc. Beware, interlocking arms in this position may dislocate shoulders and should be used with care.

Reflection

- What did you learn as pairs that helped you as you formed larger groups?
- Did you make any interesting observations about your decision-making or problem-solving processes?
- Was this primarily a physical or mental challenge? Why?

Popsicle Push-Up

Physical team challenge that demands planning & creativity.

Benefits

- Inspires creativity
- Promotes collaboration
- Develops critical-thinking
- All group sizes

People 8+

Time 20-30 mins

Instructions

1. Gather your group on an open, flat and dry surface.
2. Challenge your group to elevate the bodies of every individual off the ground for a period of five seconds, with only their hands touching the ground during this time.
3. Every person must be physically connected to the group during the five seconds.
4. No equipment or physical aids are permitted to solve the problem.
5. Allow ample time for planning, problem-solving & trial-and-error.
6. Encourage creativity, as there are many solutions.

Variations

- Challenge your group to discover as many different techniques as they can within the time limit to successfully accomplish the task.
- For large groups, form two or more smaller teams. Challenge them to work in smaller 'work stations' to ultimately solve the problem for the whole group. Typically, most groups will perceive this challenge as an 'us versus them' competition, an observation which may contribute towards a useful discussion later when the task is complete.

Reflection

- What words would you use to describe your group's process to solve the problem?
- How many ideas were generated? Were all of these attempted – why?
- What skills were leveraged the most to be successful in this exercise?

The Clock

Fast-paced, continuous improvement team-building exercise.

Benefits

- Action-packed
- Promotes collaboration
- Focus on continuous improvement
- Physical challenge

People 12+

Time 20-30 mins

Instructions

1. Form a circle sitting on the floor with everyone holding hands.
2. When ready, everyone will stand up, rotate 360 degrees in one direction and then rotate in the reverse direction.
3. To finish, everyone returns to sit on the floor in the same position they started.
4. All activity must be performed while everyone is holding hands.
5. If at any time two or more people let go of their neighbour's hands, the attempt will not count.
6. Challenge your group to perform this task as quickly as possible.
7. Provide ample time for planning, problem-solving and as many attempts as time allows.

Variations

- Challenge your group to beat a specific time (a target) which you set. On average, it takes about one second per person (plus a couple of seconds for safe measure) to complete the required moves, eg a target of 15 seconds is very doable for a group of 12 people.
- Start with people sitting in chairs (without arms.) Just beware that chairs often move in the process of people getting in and out of them.

Reflection

- In a general sense, how fast could your group possibly move?
- How would you describe your group's process to solve the task?
- How did your group accommodate the different needs of its members?

Four Pointer

Creative & physical team challenge that involves everyone.

Benefits

- Physically active
- Inspires creativity
- Fosters collaboration
- Develops critical-thinking

People 4+

Time 10-15 mins

Instructions

1. Form small teams of seven people.
2. Position each group to stand within a designated safe area.
3. Nominate a second safe area located about 15 metres away.
4. Challenge each group to move between the two areas while using no more than four anatomical points of simultaneous contact with the ground at all times.
5. Allow ample time for planning and problem-solving before the first attempt.
6. If more points of contact are made with the ground than permitted, the group starts over.
7. Continue play until all groups have traversed the area 'safely.'

Variations

- Form teams of five people, permitting only three points of contact.
- Challenge your entire group to cross the area as one wholly-connected unit, using only a mutually-agreed number of points of contact with the ground.

Reflection

- Other than physical prowess, what other challenges did you encounter in this exercise?
- How did your group attend to physical, emotional and mental safety?
- Did a sense of competition influence your performance in any way?

CHAPTER 14

Fun Community-Building Games

This final chapter features dozens of fun, interactive and engaging games that generate lots of good, positive feelings and invite everyone in your group to play at the same time.

In many cases, these games could have been classified as an ice-breaker, energiser, tag game, trust exercise or group initiative. However, they stand out on their own because they are extraordinarily FUNN activities which epitomise the essence of play.

These popular large group, community-building games feature:

- Fun as a major component
- Emphasis on play rather than competition
- Minimal rules
- Effort to minimise or avoid elimination of players
- 2 to 30 minutes of play

Just For Fun

Categories Twist – Finding Nemo – Evolution – Pruie? – Slap Bang – Wink Murder

Circle Games

Wizz Bang – Wah – Veggie Veggie – Speed Rabbit – One Duck – King Frog – Ah So Ko
Follow The Leader – Caught Ya Peekin' – The Rock – Have You Ever? – Zip Zap
Commitment – Crossed Or Uncrossed – The Man In The Moon – If You Love Me Honey, Smile

Audience Games

PDQ Test – BF Skinner – Charade Line – The Story Game
In The Manner Of The Word – Come To My Party – Bang, You're Dead

Categories Twist

Entertaining variation of classic Two Truths & Lie game.

Benefits

- Playful & fun
- Intriguing get-to-know-you game
- Inspires creativity
- Strengthens relationships

People 8+

Time 20-30 mins

Instructions

1. Form small groups of two, three or four people.
2. Each group spends 5 to 10 minutes discussing what they all have in common.
3. In conversation, each group identifies two things which all group members have in common, and one thing which is true for at least one member but not the whole group.
4. When ready, gather all groups together.
1. Taking turns, each group announces their three 'common attributes' as deadpan as possible.
2. The rest of the groups aim to identify which one of the three attributes is the lie.
3. Aim to seek consensus, but settle for a majority if necessary.
4. Finally, the nominated group reveals the correct answer.
5. Repeat this process until all groups have revealed their lie.

Variations

- Each small group presents three facts (which are in fact all true) about all group members, one for each person. The rest of the groups have to decide which fact belongs to which person.
- Individually, a person presents two truths and one lie about themselves. The rest of the group is challenged to uncover the lie.

Reflection

- How hard was it to identify interesting things in common with all others in your group?
- How unique are you, compared to others? Do you truly believe this?
- What impact does this understanding have on our self-worth and relationships with others?

Finding Nemo

Highly-interactive, fun group game with many surprises.

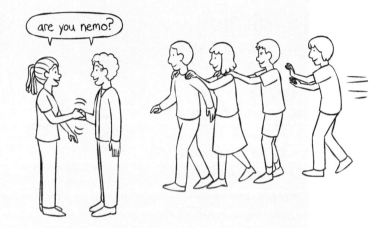

Benefits

- Addictively fun
- Highly-interactive
- Ideal for large groups
- Sharpens observation skills

People 12+

Time 10-15 mins

Instructions

1. Appoint a secret person in your group using a random method, ie this person will be 'Nemo.'
2. Everyone (including Nemo) mingles about the area greeting one another with a gentle handshake, only ever asking the question "ARE YOU NEMO?"
3. Everyone (including Nemo) must answer this question with "NO."
4. However, after greeting the first 5 – 10 people, Nemo will answer "YES" to everyone.
5. When a person receives a "YES" to their question, they are invited to quickly and silently form a conga-line behind Nemo.
6. Everyone aims to form a part of the conga-line, yet avoid being the last person to join it.
7. It is not necessary for an individual to shake the hands of Nemo to join the conga-line.
8. The game concludes once everyone becomes a part of the line.
9. Play several rounds, or try a variation.

Variations

- For large groups, form two or more smaller groups of 20+ people, each of them finding a Nemo. Eliminate the last 4 to 8 people standing at the back of the line, and invite them to join one of the other groups to continue play.
- Appoint a secret 'Bruce' (the shark) character at the same time as Nemo. Game is played as normal. Once the line has formed, ask Bruce to identify themselves, and eliminate everyone who is standing behind Bruce.

Reflection

- How did it feel to discover you were the first person to join the conga-line?
- How did it feel to be the last person to join the conga-line?
- Are these feelings the same as when you are or are not part of the 'in group?'

Evolution

Fun, chaotic & highly-interactive community-building game.

Benefits

- Very playful & fun
- Highly-interactive
- Promotes critical-thinking
- Ideal for large groups

People 12+

Time 5-10 mins

Instructions

1. Introduce five animated creatures, each with a unique physical stance and sound, eg:
   - Egg – crouch down into a little ball with legs, and make muffled "EEK-EEK" sounds.
   - Chicken – flap your arms by your sides and make clucking sounds.
   - Dinosaur – raise your arms above your head, take big heavy strides and make scary noises.
   - Ninja Turtle – make like a kung-fu champion slicing the air with lots of karate chops.
   - Supreme Being – fold your arms like a genie, look calm and wise.
2. Everyone aims to become a Supreme Being.
3. When play begins, everyone starts at the lowest level (the egg.)
4. To progress through the five phases, each creature must find another like-creature and play a quick round of Rock-Paper-Scissors.
5. The 'winner' steps up one evolutionary phase, and the 'loser' will drop down a phase.
6. In the case of two eggs facing-off, the 'loser' remains an egg.
7. Play for a minute or two, or until the energy starts to wane.

Variations

- Identify five areas within your playing space where people of a similar genealogy exist and play, ie start in first area as eggs, then winners move to next area, etc.
- Substitute the Rock-Paper-Scissors format with any other competitive element, eg toss of a coin (heads win,) randomly selecting a card from a deck of playing cards (highest value wins,) playing a round of **Slap Bang** (winner advances,) etc.

Reflection

- How did it feel to frequently drop-back to the lower levels of evolution? Why?
- How did it feel to become a Supreme Being? Why?
- Does this game mirror certain behaviours and patterns in our life?

Pruie?

Highly-sensory, interactive & absorbing group game.

Benefits

- Addictively fun
- Promotes critical-thinking
- Develops trust & empathy
- Ideal for large groups

People 12+

Time 10-15 mins

Instructions

1. Gather your group in a large, open, flat space.
2. Appoint a secret person in your group using a random method, ie this person will be 'Pruie.'
3. To start, everyone (including Pruie) closes their eyes, raises their hands in the Bumpers Up position and mingles with one another.
4. Every time someone bumps into another person, they say "PRUIE?"
5. If both people respond with "PRUIE" they will continue on their journey.
6. When an individual does not respond, the silent person is the Pruie, and the enquirer should immediately link arms with them.
7. Everyone aims to locate and link arms with Pruie as soon as possible, thereby becoming a part of the Pruie, ie they, too, no longer respond to others who bump into them.
8. No words, other than "PRUIE" may be uttered at any time during the game.
9. As more people become a part of the Pruie, they remain silent with their eyes closed.
10. Play continues until everyone becomes a part of the Pruie.
11. Finally, invite your group to open their eyes, and share their various stories.

Variations

- Adopt another nonsensical (or meaningful) word as the name of the initial, silent and elusive person.
- For particularly large groups, appoint two or three Pruies.

Reflection

- How did it feel when you found Pruie?
- How did it feel to be one of the last people to find Pruie?
- Describe a time in your life when you were (or were not) part of the 'in' group.

Slap Bang

*Highly-focused, energetic &
fun partner-duelling game.*

Benefits

- Playful
- Energising
- Rock-Paper-Scissors variation
- Promotes critical-thinking

People 2+

Time 2-5 mins

Instructions

1. Form into pairs, standing a metre apart from each other.
2. Establish (and practice for 5 seconds) a beat by slapping open hands on thighs, about once per second.
3. Introduce three unique physical gestures, asking your group to mimic them one at a time:
    - Safe: arms crossed on chest and fingers resting on shoulders;
    - Loading: with fingers clenched and thumbs pointing over the top of your shoulders; and
    - Bang: with both hands forming a gun-like gesture in front of the body.
4. Between beats, an individual will strategically play one of these three gestures – Safe, Loading or Bang.
5. Safe and Loading gestures can be played at any time, but Bang may only be played directly after Loading.
6. When ready, each pair resumes the beat.
7. In each round, an individual aims to win by playing Bang at the same time their partner plays Loading.
8. All other combinations of gestures produce no result, so the beat will continue until a win is secured.
9. Play several rounds over 2 to 3 minutes, and then swap partners.

Variations

- Form a circle. On a predictable, possibly slower beat, each person assumes one of the three poses. All those who chose to 'Bang' will aim directly at one person across the other side of the circle, and if the latter is 'Loading,' this person is eliminated. Each person aims to be the last person standing.

- Re-frame each of the three gestures to produce a positive result. For example, the Safe gesture means 'I'm happy at home,' the Loading gesture means 'Come out to play,' and the Bang gesture means 'Okay.' An individual scores a point each time their 'Okay' meets their partner's 'Come out to play.'

Reflection

- Describe your level of competence in the beginning.
- Was it difficult to focus on both your own and your partner's moves at the same time? Why?
- Where else do you try to do two things at once?

Wink Murder

Highly-interactive & secretive elimination group game.

Benefits
- Very playful
- Engaging
- Inspires creativity
- Multiple variations

People 12+
Time 15-20 mins

Instructions

1. Use a random method to secretly appoint an 'assassin.'
2. The assassin's weapon of choice is a wink of their eye.
3. The assassin's ultimate goal is to eliminate everyone in the group as quickly as possible, by winking discretely at each person.
4. The rest of the group aims to catch the assassin doing their dirty work.
5. Over the course of several minutes, everyone mingles and greets one another as they pass with a smile and a look in the eye as often as possible.
6. When an individual catches a wink from the assassin, they must wait at least five seconds (as the continue to mingle) before dying a histrionic death, and removing themselves from the action.
7. The assassin is not obliged to wink at everyone they greet.

8. If someone suspects who the assassin is, they may raise their hand and shout "I ACCUSE." At this point, everyone stops mingling and waits for a second person to raise their hand as a seconder. If a second accuser does not appear, the game continues.

9. If an accuser attracts the interest of a seconder, on your count of "1, 2, 3" each accuser must point directly to who they believe to be the assassin. This will cause one of three results:

    - If they point at different people, regardless if one of them is correct, they are both eliminated.

    - If they both point at the wrong person, they are both eliminated.

    - If they both point at the (correct) assassin, the game will end.

10. No one is permitted to communicate or otherwise indicate to others who they believe may be the assassin.

11. Play continues until either everyone is eliminated, or two people make a successful accusation.

12. Play several rounds, randomly appointing a new assassin with each round.

Variations

- Everyone mingles and shakes hands as they greet one another. The assassin shakes hands in a peculiar way, eg with index finger pointed forward and pressing or rubbing the wrist of their hand-shaking partner.

- The assassin directs a subtle kiss of their pursed lips to those he or she wishes to eliminate. Once kissed, people swoon to their death with a giant exasperated sigh as if falling deeply in love.

Reflection

- Was it difficult to identify the assassin? Why or why not?

- As the assassin, did you manage to conceal your intentions successfully? How?

- What subtle changes did you notice in someone to make you think they could be an assassin?

Wizz Bang

Fun, fast-paced & expressive community-building game.

Benefits

- Very playful & fun
- Fosters critical-thinking
- Develops collaboration
- Sharpens observation skills

People 12+

Time 5-10 mins

Instructions

1. Form a circle, including yourself, with people standing close to their neighbours.
2. Your group's goal is to pass an imaginary impulse around the group as fast and as accurately as possible.
3. To start, flick your hand rapidly in front of you as you say "WIZZ" causing the impulse to travel to your left (or right) neighbour.
4. Upon receiving a 'Wizz,' an individual has two options:
   - Flick their hand and call 'WIZZ' allowing the impulse to travel in the same direction; or
   - Thrust their forearm vertically in front of themselves and say "BANG" causing the impulse to reverse direction.
5. Once started, the imaginary impulse will travel in both directions around the circle.
6. After 30 seconds has elapsed, introduce one and eventually both of the following pairs of gestures into the game:
   - Vroom: sends the impulse anywhere in the circle by rapidly extending one's arms towards the direction of a random person in the circle and saying "VROOM." Must receive an 'Ahhhh' in response.
   - Ahhhh: receives a 'Vroom' by holding one's arms and hands as if catching an object, and then quickly nursing the imaginary impulse into their chest, and saying "AHHHH."
   - Shoot: sends the impulse anywhere in the circle as if it was a basketball, holding one's arms up high, flicking their fingers forward and shooting for a goal, saying "SHOOT." Must receive a 'Kerplunk' in response.
   - Kerplunk: receives the 'Shoot' by forming a ring with one's arms, and upon watching the imaginary impulse swish through, calls out "KERPLUNK."

7. Upon completing an 'Ahhhh' or a 'Kerplunk' an individual may 'Wizz,' 'Vroom' or 'Shoot.'

8. Continue playing until your group's interest is piqued.

Variations

- Create your own methods of motion, or invite your group to invent a series of interesting gestures and sounds.
- Introduce the game as an elimination, whereby anyone making a mistake or taking too long to respond is 'outta the game.'

Reflection

- What was the hardest part of the exercise?
- Did you ever make a mistake? On these occasions, what did you say to yourself?
- What skills were required to pass the impulse quickly and accurately?

Wah

Playful & energetic circle game to fill-in two minutes.

Benefits

- Very playful & fun
- Ideal time-filler
- Promotes collaboration
- Develops critical-thinking

People 8+

Time 5-10 mins

Instructions

1. Form a circle of 8 to 12 people, including yourself, facing into the centre.

2. To start, point your two arms with palms pressed together towards a person on the other side of the circle as you loudly call out "WAH!"

3. This newly appointed person (warrior) must immediately raise their two arms above their head – with palms pressed together – and call out "WAH!"

4. Next, the two neighbours of the warrior must immediately swing their pressed-together palms towards (but not touching) the stomach of the warrior and call out "WAH!"

5. Finally, the warrior lowers their arms, with palms pressed together, towards a new person in the circle, calling out "WAH!" to nominate a new warrior.

6. This routine continues over and over around the circle.

7. Explain that maintaining a consistent rhythm of swift actions and "WAH's" is the key.

8. When an error is made, or a response is too slow, invite the person responsible to become the new warrior.

9. Continue play for several minutes, or try a variation.

Variations

- Eliminate those who respond too slowly or perform the wrong action. Continue playing until two people remain in the circle (impossible to play any further) and crown them winners.

- Start with two or more circles. Invite those who are eliminated to join another circle, thus giving the game longevity. For ease of play, all new members to a circle should wait until there is a pause in play (owing to an error) before joining the circle to play a new round.

Reflection

- What surprised you about this activity?

- How easy was it for you to focus on the action and respond in an accurate and timely manner?

- Did you have fun? Why?

Too much fun is never enough

Veggie Veggie

Nonsensical group game
guaranteed to make people laugh.

Benefits

- Very playful & fun
- Generates laughter
- Sharpens listening skills
- Circle game

People 8+

Time 5-10 mins

Instructions

1. Form a circle, including yourself.
2. Each person thinks of a vegetable and shares it with the rest of the group (to ensure there are no duplicates.)
3. Once started, all talking must occur with one's lips curled over their teeth (so no teeth can be seen.)
4. When ready, one person will call out the name of their vegetable twice, and then follow it up with the name of someone else's vegetable twice, eg "PUMPKIN-PUMPKIN, TOMATO-TOMATO."
5. The person who chose the second-named vegetable, must quickly respond by saying the name of their vegetable twice, and then follow immediately with the name of another person's vegetable, and so on.
6. This process continues randomly among members of your group.
7. Your group aims to maintain an accurate and steady beat for as long as possible.
8. When an individual shows their teeth or takes too long to respond when it's their turn to talk, the action stops.
9. Once the laughter subsides, the neighbour to the left of the person who made the 'mistake' will start a new round.
10. Continue play for several minutes.

Variations

- Whenever an individual makes a mistake (shows their teeth, responds too slowly, etc) they are eliminated from the circle. Play continues once the circle re-joins, until two people remain.

- Introduce any category you choose, such as fruits, motor vehicles, countries, people's names, etc.

Reflection

- How did you feel when you first had to speak with your lips curled over your teeth?
- Did your comprehension improve with practice?
- What other difficult task have you accomplished in your life that improved with practice?

Speed Rabbit

Playful, interactive & energetic community-building game.

Benefits

- Very playful & fun
- Highly-interactive
- Develops critical-thinking
- Promotes collaboration

People 12+

Time 10-15 mins

Instructions

1. Form a circle, with you standing in the middle.
2. Establish a series of unique physical gestures and sounds which create the form of three animals, each involving three people. For example:
   - Elephant: one person uses their arms to create a trunk, while their two neighbours circle their arms to the side to create large ears;
   - Cow: one person interlocks fingers and turns their hands upside down to point their thumbs down, while their two neighbours each grab one of these thumbs as if milking them: and
   - Kangaroo: one person forms a pouch using their arms in front of themselves, while their two neighbours lean on this person's closest shoulder and thump their outside legs.
3. To start, randomly point to one person in the circle and call out the name of one of the three animals, and quickly count to ten.

4. Immediately, this person and their two neighbours, must arrange their bodies to look like the animal, making the appropriate sound, before you get to "...TEN."

5. If one of the three people in the circle makes a mistake, or is too slow, the most deserving person is invited to swap positions with you in the middle of the circle.

6. After several minutes, add extra people in the centre of the circle, or try a variation.

Variations

- Introduce a fourth or even fifth animal. Make them distinctly different, ie even if every animal has ears, make sure they are not similar to each other.

- Experiment with other forms, such as occupations, famous people, sports or corporate attributes.

Reflection

- How often did you make a mistake? How did it happen?

- What was the consequence of making a mistake?

- In our ordinary lives, are we encouraged to make mistakes, or not?

One Duck

Contagiously fun game that triggers bursts of laughter.

Benefits

- Simple
- Great time-filler
- Demands critical-thinking
- Ideal for small groups

People 8+

Time 10-15 mins

Instructions

1. Form a circle.

2. Ask your group to repeat the words of a four-part stanza - "ONE DUCK – FELL IN – THE POND – KERPLUNK."

3. Repeat the verse, one person at a time in a clockwise direction around the circle, saying one part of the stanza each.

4. Once complete, the next person in the circle re-starts the verse, but now, each part of the stanza is repeated by two people in a row, eg one says "ONE DUCK" and their neighbour says "ONE DUCK" and the next person says "FELL IN.." etc.

5. Next, the full stanza continues around the circle with each part repeated by three people in a row, then four people in a row, and finally five people in a row.

6. A round ends when someone makes a mistake, or pauses for too long before adding to the sequence.

7. When a mistake is made, the next-in-line starts a new round with a confident "ONE DUCK."

8. Challenge your group to successfully recite each of the four parts of the stanza by five people in a row in a single round.

9. Continue play for as many rounds as your group's focus will allow.

Variations

• When each of the stanzas is complete, instruct your group to recite the next stanza in the opposite direction. This option works very well with small groups of 5 to 10 people.

• When an individual makes a mistake or pauses too long before adding to the correct sequence of phrases, they are eliminated from the circle. Play continues until you have two people remaining – way too much fun!

Reflection

• Why is the pinnacle of this task so difficult to complete successfully?

• What did you notice when someone made a mistake?

• How do you create an atmosphere in which people are willing to 'have a go?'

Connection before content will amplify your success

King Frog

Creatively playful game that triggers bursts of laughter.

Benefits

- Very playful
- Addictively fun
- Inspires creativity
- Promotes critical-thinking

People 8+

Time 20-30 mins

Instructions

1. Sit in a circle, including yourself, whereby everyone can see everyone else.
2. Each person thinks of a unique action and sound which mimics an animal, eg gorilla beating its chest.
3. In turn, rotate around the circle to introduce everyone's gesture and sound, starting with you.
4. As leader, introduce yourself as King Frog, as you move one palm swiftly over the palm of your other hand away from you (as if a frog was jumping off a lily pad.)
5. Mimic the gesture and sound of each animal as they are introduced around the circle, one at a time.
6. Each round starts with King Frog performing their action, followed immediately with the gesture and sound of another animal.
7. This will instruct the person who is represented by that (second) animal to respond by quickly doing their action and follow it with the actions of another animal, and so on.
8. Encourage your group to maintain the rhythm of the gestures and sounds as quick and accurate as possible.
9. If someone makes a mistake, or is too slow to respond, they must leave their seat and sit directly to the left of King Frog, meaning everyone in between moves to the empty seat on their left.
10. Importantly, when someone moves into a new seat, they will assume the animal that originated in that seat, ie players do not take their animal with them.
11. Each individual aims to move steadily around the circle until they arrive in the King Frog's seat.
12. Play as many rounds as your group has the energy.

Variations

- Introduce an elimination format, so that when someone makes a mistake, they leave the circle. King Frog starts the first round, after which, the person to the left of whoever was just eliminated, resumes the action within five seconds. No one moves seats, it's simply a matter of survival of the fittest.
- Use people's names. So, Jimmy starts with "Jimmy-Jimmy, Jane-Jane," and then Jane replies with "Jane-Jane, Sanchez-Sanchez," and so on.

Reflection

- What strategies did you employ to avoid making a mistake?
- Which were the most difficult animals to remember or perform? Why?
- Was it worth the effort to become King Frog?

Ah So Ko

Extremely engaging & playful circle game just for fun.

Benefits

- Creative
- Sharpens reflexes
- Promotes critical-thinking
- Generates energy

People 8+

Time 15-20 mins

Instructions

1. Sit your group in a circle, so that everyone can see each other with ease.
2. Introduce three unique gestures and sounds:
   - Strike one hand quickly under your chin and say a loud "AH."
   - Strike one hand directly above your head and say a loud "SO."
   - Finally, strike one hand directly in front of you and say a loud "KO."
3. "AH SO KO" are always uttered in this sequence, but by one person at a time.
4. Indicate that with each strike of a hand, a new person is signalled to give the next gesture.

5. To begin, one person says "AH" as they point with their hand to their left or right neighbour.

6. This neighbour must quickly say "SO" as they point with their hand toward their left or right neighbour.

7. This neighbour must quickly say "KO" and point directly at any other person in the circle.

8. The person to whom is pointed will restart the sequence from "AH."

9. This sequence repeats itself over and over until someone makes a mistake.

10. Upon a mistake, the group extends their clenched fists towards the centre of the circle, with thumbs pointed up and moving them over their shoulders, shouting "YOU'RE OUTTA THE GAME" to whoever made the error.

11. The eliminated person will leave the circle and become a 'heckler' by distracting others hoping to cause them to make a mistake too.

12. Meanwhile, the circle re-joins, and the person to the left of the one who withdrew must restart the sequence from "AH" within three seconds.

13. Game continues until one person remains.

Variations

- When a person is eliminated, they are invited to become a heckler. This means that they can do (almost) anything – other than touch or obstruct the view of others - to distract them so that they, too, may make a mistake.

- Add a fourth gesture – "NO." This gesture follows directly after "KO" and is performed by the person to whom "KO" is given. However, note that "NO" is purely optional. So, the person receiving "KO" may choose to follow on with "AH," or they can place both of their hands in front of their face and say "NO," which like a mirror causes the "KO" to be returned to whomever delivered it. In this latter case, the person who had delivered "KO" must respond to the subsequent "NO" with an "AH" and the game continues.

Reflection

- Was this game fun to play? Why or why not?

- What did you notice as the activity progressed?

- What difference does enthusiasm make to our work, home, school and play?

Follow The Leader

Curious, interactive & entertaining guessing game.

Benefits

- Very playful
- Physically active
- Sharpens observation skills
- Promotes critical-thinking

People 12+

Time 10-15 mins

Instructions

1. Form a circle.
2. One person volunteers to be the first 'observer' and then closes their eyes.
3. Meanwhile, the rest of your group silently points to one other person in the circle to become the 'leader.'
4. While the observer has their eyes closed, instruct the leader to start making a series of random movements.
5. The rest of the group will imitate these movements, as soon and as often as they occur.
6. Now, ask the observer to open their eyes and move into the centre of the circle.
7. The observer's goal is to identify who is initiating the series of moves (leader) in less than five guesses.
8. Encourage the 'leader' to frequently change their movements.
9. Continue play for several rounds, allowing new people to be the observer and leader.

Variations

- Invite your group (including the leader) to mingle within a pre-defined space allowing the observer to move in and out of the group, too.
- For high-performance groups, ask the leader to be a 'statue,' moving from one frozen position to another. Hint, best time to move is when the observer isn't looking.

Reflection

- How did it feel to be the observer, especially if it took you a long time to identify the leader?
- How did it feel to watch someone struggle to identify the leader?
- In our experience, what allowed this game to be fun?

Caught Ya Peekin'

Very playful energiser that generates lots of laughter.

Benefits

- Quick
- Very playful
- Great time-filler
- Promotes critical-thinking

People 8+

Time 2-5 mins

Instructions

1. Form a circle (sitting or standing) whereby every person can clearly see every other person.

2. Without further instruction, ask everyone to close their eyes.

3. Each person may open their eyes, at any time, in an attempt to catch another person with their eyes open too.

4. To eliminate a person caught with their eyes open, an individual must call out "CAUGHT YA PEEKIN' ..." followed by that person's name.

5. If a person is successfully eliminated, invite them to open their eyes and put their hands on their head, or to push out of the circle.

6. Each individual aims to stay in the game for as long as possible.

7. Continue playing until a winner emerges, or move on when the energy starts to wane.

Variations

- To encourage lots of peeking, grant each person three lives.

- To prevent some sneaky people just sitting with their eyes closed the whole game, introduce the rule that everyone must open their eyes at least once every 10 to 15 seconds.

Reflection

- Did you feel silly sitting in a group with your eyes closed? Why?
- How did it feel to get caught by another person you weren't looking at?
- What skills are involved in this game? What about trust?

The Rock

Fascinating group game that sharpens observation skills.

Benefits

- Gentle, yet fun
- Develops critical-thinking
- Sharpens observation skills
- Focus on connections

People 8+

Time 20-30 mins

Instructions

1. Form a circle, facing into the centre.
2. Everyone closes their eyes and clenches both of their hands behind their backs.
3. If someone is willing to receive the 'rock,' they should open one of their hands in a receiving position.
4. Walk around the group and secretly deposit a small stone into one person's open hand.
5. Next, everyone brings their clenched hands in front of them, opens their eyes, and quietly and comfortably sits down with their hands visible to all.
6. Everyone starts observing others in the group, silently, with the aim to identify the person who is holding the 'rock.'
7. After 20 seconds of silent observation, invite one or more people to raise their hands, and nominate who they think is holding the rock.
8. Each person gets one chance to make a nomination.
9. If the guess is correct, the game is over. Otherwise, the guesser is eliminated from the group and will push out of the circle.
10. At the conclusion of each round, pause for a brief reflection to review successful nominations.
11. Play as many rounds as your group has interest.

Variation

- In advance, tell your group that you may or may not deposit the stone in someone's hand. With each round, every individual aims to identify (a) if the stone has been deposited in the hands of a group member, or not and (b) who is holding it, which of course, now includes you.

Reflection

- What sorts of changes did you observe that may suggest someone was holding the rock?
- Did your senses sharpen as each round progressed? How?
- What difference can you feel in the group at the end of the game, compared to the beginning?

Have You Ever?

Hilarious, interactive, get-to-know-you-more circle game.

Benefits

- Very entertaining
- Promotes communication
- Fosters creativity
- Engaging

People 12+

Time 15-20 mins

Instructions

1. Form a circle, with each person standing on a spot (or sitting in a chair.)
2. Move yourself to stand in the centre of the circle (you are without a seat).
3. Ask a question that starts with "HAVE YOU EVER...?" eg "... BEEN TO THAILAND?"
4. Everyone in the circle who can answer 'Yes' to the question may choose to leave their spot, and attempt to fill a vacant spot elsewhere in the circle.
5. No one may move into the spot of their immediate left or right neighbours.
6. The person asking the question will also attempt to fill a spot as it becomes vacant.
7. Once every vacant spot has been filled, the person without a spot will ask the next "HAVE YOU EVER...?" question.
8. If someone can not think of a question, or simply does not want to be in the centre, they may invite a volunteer to swap roles with them.
9. Continue playing until the energy of your group starts to wane.

Variations

- Narrow the scope of the experiences your group may ask questions about, such as "HAVE YOU EVER….. AT SCHOOL?", or "HAVE YOU EVER….. WITH YOUR FRIENDS?"

- Everyone has a 'spot' and may ask a "HAVE YOU EVER…?" question at any time. In this case, everyone to whom the question applies is invited into the centre of the circle to join in a rousing chorus of - slap-slap (of thighs,) clap-clap (of hands,) click-click (of fingers,) "YEAAAHHHHH" (sung gloriously.) All return to their spots and a new person volunteers the next question, and so on.

Reflection

- Can you think of at least two new things you learned about others in this game?

- Was it difficult for you to think of something interesting to ask? Why?

- What cultural norms are necessary to help people feel confident and safe to share?

Zip Zap

Very playful, highly-interactive & energising group game.

Benefits

- Fun
- Highly-interactive
- Generates energy
- Sharpens focus & reflexes

People 12+

Time 5-10 mins

Instructions

1. Form a circle, facing into the centre, with you standing in the middle.

2. To start, use both arms and hands pressed together in front of you to randomly point to one person in the circle.

3. As you point, say "ZIP" which will prompt this person to immediately crouch to the ground.

4. The two neighbours of this person will immediately turn to face one another and quickly place the back of their own wrist on their forehead with fingers pointing to the other person as quickly as possible.

5. If the pointed-at person and their neighbours respond quickly and accurately, they each survive to play another round.

6. However, if one of these three people are too slow or make an error, they are invited to swap roles with you, to become the new person in the centre.

7. Play a couple of 'test' rounds to help your group understand what's expected, before play begins.

8. After a few minutes, introduce one or more new people into the middle of the circle.

Variations

- Substitute the 'zip' and 'zap' with the names of the people being pointed to. For example, as the person in the middle of the circle, you say the name of the person you're pointing to (and they say yours,) and the two neighbours say the other neighbour's name.

- The person in the centre ('pointer') remains there all the time, and continues zipping until the final two people are left standing.

Reflection

- What caused you to laugh during this exercise? Why?

- On a scale of 1 to 10, with 10 being highest, how would you rate your ability to react quickly?

- Where else in our lives do we need to react quickly?

A good idea doesn't care who it belongs to

Commitment

*Quick-movement energiser
to teach safety consciousness.*

Benefits

- Fast-paced
- Highly-energetic
- Sharpens observation skills
- Promotes collaboration

People 12+

Time 10-15 mins

Instructions

1. Form a large circle, with each person standing on a 'spot,' eg shoe, chalk-mark.
2. Place yourself in the centre of the circle (you do not have a spot.)
3. An individual may, at any time, swap spots with another person standing on the other side of the circle, while attempting to prevent the person in the centre of the circle (you) from stealing an empty spot.
4. Each person aims to swap to a new spot as many times as possible in the time allocated.
5. When both spots are re-occupied, the person who is left stranded without a spot becomes the new person in the centre of the circle.
6. Alert your group to the possibility of collisions, whereby all movements should aim to avoid contact with other people.
7. Continue playing until the time has expired, or the energy of your group starts to wane.

Variations

- Allow anyone from anywhere to fill a spot that is unoccupied, eg when two people have committed to swap their spots, one of their neighbours may simply step across and steal one of them. Of course, the centre person is still plotting to steal anyone's spot at any time.
- Instruct everyone to make a move to swap spots at least once every 30 seconds. This invitation will encourage a few of the more hesitant folk to have a go, and ramp up the fun.

Reflection

- What did it take for you to consider moving off your 'safe' spot?
- How easy was it to commit? What stopped/helped you to move forward?
- What might this exercise teach us about making commitments?

Crossed Or Uncrossed

Lateral-thinking game to strengthen observation skills.

Benefits

- Simple, but not easy
- Develops critical-thinking
- Promotes creativity
- Sharpens observation skills

People 4+

Time 15-20 mins

Instructions

1. Sit in a circle, including yourself.
2. Each person aims to identify what the 'key' is to unlock the secret to this puzzle.
3. Sitting with your legs crossed, pass two sticks to the person on your left (or right) and say "I PASS THESE STICKS TO YOU CROSSED. HOW DO YOU RECEIVE THEM?"
4. As your neighbour receives the sticks, they are required to respond that they are either receiving them crossed or uncrossed (there are only two options.)
5. Then, invite your neighbour to repeat your example, and pass the sticks to their neighbour, and so on.
6. This is the key: No matter how the sticks are positioned as they are passed, or received, the 'key' will always be related to how the legs of the people are situated at the moment they pass or receive the sticks.
7. For example, the sticks you receive may in fact be crossed, but you will say "I RECEIVE THEM UNCROSSED" if at that moment your legs are uncrossed.
8. As the sticks are passed, correct any flawed responses.
9. Continue to offer more and more obvious clues until everyone has identified the key.

Variation

- Take a look at **The Man In The Moon**, **Come To My Party** and **Bang, You're Dead**.

Reflection

- Did it take you a long time to figure out what the key was?
- How did you feel during the game, especially when you didn't know the key?
- What is the likely outcome when people do not feel a part of the group?

The Man In The Moon

Fun lateral-thinking exercise with a focus on subtlety.

Benefits

- Simple, but not easy
- Develops critical-thinking
- Promotes creativity
- Sharpens observation skills

People 4+

Time 10-15 mins

Instructions

1. Sit in a circle, including yourself.
2. Each person aims to identify what the 'key' is to unlock the secret to this puzzle.
3. Use your index finger to draw a circle in the air in front of you, and then add two eyes, a nose and a mouth.
4. As you draw, subtly clear your throat and then say "THE MAN IN THE MOON HAS TWO EYES, A NOSE AND A MOUTH."
5. Next, invite a series of volunteers to repeat exactly what you did.
6. Here's the key: subtly clear your throat just before you start drawing.
7. Unless a person clears their throat before commencing their attempt, they will not have unlocked the secret key.
8. As each person makes an attempt to uncover the key, congratulate those who get it, and encourage those who do not.
9. Continue to offer more and more obvious clues until everyone has identified the key.

Variation

- Vary the key, eg interlock your fingers in front of you as soon as you have finished drawing.

Reflection

- How did you feel during the exercise, especially when you finally unlocked the key?
- What did you notice among other members of the group who had not unlocked the key?
- What did these behaviours communicate to you?

If You Love Me Honey, Smile

Very entertaining group game to test one's determination.

Benefits

- Very playful & fun
- Generates lots of laughter
- Inspires creativity
- Builds community

People 12+

Time 10-15 mins

Instructions

1. Form a circle, either standing or seated in chairs (not including you.)
2. To start, stand in the centre of the circle.
3. Your goal is to invite someone from the circle to leave their seat by making them smile.
4. To achieve this goal, approach and face one person at a time and say the words "IF YOU LOVE ME HONEY, SMILE."
5. If the candidate smiles, they are invited to swap roles with you in the middle.
6. If the candidate does not smile, you must approach a new candidate, and try again.
7. Continue playing for many rounds, involving multiple people to try their luck in the middle.

Variations

- For a more challenging predicament, the unseated person is not permitted to touch anyone.
- Both people must never show their teeth when they talk, ie they curl their lips over their teeth as they speak. If glistening teeth are revealed by either party, the concordant penalty is applied.

Reflection

- On a scale of 1 to 10, how strong would you describe your determination not to smile?
- What strategies did you employ to not smile? Were you successful?
- What caused your 'poker face' to crack?

PDQ Test

Hilarious whole-group exercise involving quirky movements.

Benefits

- Very playful & fun
- Inspires creativity
- Celebrates diversity
- Ideal time-filler

People 2+

Time 10-15 mins

Instructions

1. Assemble your group in front of you, sitting or standing.
2. Introduce the idea that you are about to demonstrate a series of physical 'tests' which you would like each person to attempt.
3. This is a self-assessed test, and only the individual will know if they passed or not.
4. Start by clicking your fingers, first your dominant and then less-dominant hands/fingers.
5. Next, invite everyone to attempt to whistle through their lips, and then pop their cheeks with a finger, perform a **Wiggle Waggle**, etc.
6. Demonstrate as many nonsensical 'tests' as you can perform yourself.
7. Conclude by inviting one or more volunteers to demonstrate a unique 'test' which they can successfully perform.

Variations

- Poke out your tongue and curl its sides so that it looks a bit like the letter U. Can you do it the other way, ie an upside down U?
- Extend your two index fingers in front of you so that they touch end to end, then look at the point at which these two fingers touch, and notice the linked sausage. See it? If you can't, try looking beyond your fingers (and not at them) and the linked sausage will suddenly jump out at you (somewhat blurred perhaps.) Then, pull your fingers away from each other slightly, and voila! You'll observe a rack of floating human finger sausages!

Reflection

- Did you pass the test? Does a 'pass' matter?
- Which movement or action did you think was the most bizarre?
- Did you feel silly performing some of the moves? Why?

BF Skinner

Extremely fun & creative audience participation exercise.

Benefits

- Very entertaining
- Inspires creativity
- Generates lots of laughter
- Audience participation

People 12+

Time 20-30 mins

Instructions

1. Assemble your group in an area with ample room to move in front.
2. Ask two volunteers to leave the space, so that they can not hear or see what is happening.
3. While the pair are absent, ask the rest of your group to agree on a unique physical position involving two people, eg standing back to back with hands on heads.
4. Invite the volunteers to return in front of your group.
5. The pair now work together as they move their bodies to discover the unknown physical position.
6. The group is not permitted to speak to the pair.
7. Use only the group's applause to encourage (and discourage) the pair as they get closer (and further away) from the desired position.
8. Faster, more enthusiastic clapping means the pair is getting closer, and slower, less energetic applause means they are not close to the desired position.
9. Allow up to five minutes of trial-and-error before introducing subtle clues to guide their efforts.
10. As soon as the pair achieve the desired position (or close thereto) lead the group in wild ecstatic applause.
11. Continue play with more volunteer pairs.

Variations

- Involve three or four people to create a position in which every person is physically connected in some way to the others.
- Take a look at **In The Manner Of The Word** for more delightful, audience-participation fun.

Reflection

- What emotions did you experience during this activity?
- Did you get frustrated? If so, how did you respond to this feeling?
- Describe your experience of being coached by the applause of the group. Was this useful?

Charade Line

Entertaining story-telling exercise that audiences love.

Benefits

- Very playful & fun
- Inspires creativity
- Promotes communication
- Sharpens observation skills

People   12+

Time   20-30 mins

Instructions

1. Gather your group, facing a 'performance area.'
2. Ask five volunteers to form a straight line facing side-on to the group, standing about a metre apart from each other.
3. Tap the closest volunteer on the shoulder, inviting them to turn around and face you.
4. Proceed to mime a 20 to 30 second story which features lots of action, intricate movements, use of imaginary props, etc.
5. As the 'story-teller,' you can not speak or use any verbal communication whatsoever.
6. Other than the audience, only the first person you tapped will have witnessed your story.
7. Once your story is complete, the first volunteer taps the shoulder of the next person in line and proceeds to re-tell the story as best as they can remember it.
8. This process of re-telling the story continues all the way down the line until the fifth and final person witnesses the story.
9. The story-teller may only mime their story once.

10. For fun, ask each person starting from the very last person to explain what they saw happening in the story.

11. Conclude by performing the original story again, mostly for the benefit of your group of volunteers.

Variations

- Invite two people to mime a story to another pair, the first in a line of pairs. Allow some thinking time for the initial story-tellers to develop their story.

- Each person mimes the actions and gestures of a chosen occupation, eg baker, plumber, dentist, zoo-keeper, etc. At the conclusion of the mines, ask each person (starting from the last) to identify the occupation they saw demonstrated before them.

Reflection

- How much fun was it to watch the stories being told as an audience member?

- If you formed part of the line, how did you feel as the story unfolded?

- What can we learn about effective communication in this exercise?

The Story Game

Hilarious story-telling game to involve the whole group.

Benefits

- Very entertaining
- Inspires creativity
- Triggers bursts of laughter
- Audience participation

People 12+
Time 15-20 mins

Instructions

1. Gather your group together.

2. Explain that one person will aim to retell a story which the rest of the group has created without their input.

3. To start, ask one person to leave the room, to a space where they can not hear what is being discussed by the rest of the group.

4. Upon the volunteer's absence, ask your group to nominate two 'things' - one ending with a vowel and the other ending with a consonant, eg kangaroo and train or Mumbai and sandwich, etc.

5. This is the story: when the volunteer asks a question, if the last word ends with a consonant, the group must answer "YES" and if it ends with a vowel, the group must answer "NO."

6. Invite the story-teller to return to the group, and inform them that the story involves the two 'things' nominated by the group.

7. The story-teller may only ask questions which can be answered with a "YES" or "NO" response.

8. The story-teller starts by asking their first question, to re-create the story.

9. Encourage the story-teller to keep the story moving, to create a beginning, middle and an end to the story.

10. Allow the story-telling to continue for 10 to 15 minutes.

11. At a point when the story appears to have reached a conclusion, lead your group into rapturous applause.

12. Finally, reveal the true story was based on the last letter of each of the story-teller's questions.

Variations

• Invite two people to become the story-tellers. This is possibly even more hilarious, as you observe the interplay between the two story-tellers.

• Take a look at **Charade Line** to enjoy an equally enthralling, story-telling group experience.

Reflection

• How did it feel to be the story-teller, at different points along the time-line?

• What observations did you, as a group, make of the story-teller?

• Did you, as part of the group, ever feel a guilty pleasure? Why?

In The Manner Of The Word

Entertaining guessing-game to sharpen communication skills.

Benefits

- Playful & fun
- Inspires creativity
- Audience participation
- Develops communication skills

People 12+

Time 5-10 mins

Instructions

1. Invite one or more volunteers to stand in front of the rest of your group.
2. Allow 10 seconds, for the volunteer(s) to secretly choose one adverb, eg slowly, nervously, quietly.
3. To start, the rest of your group offers the first of a series of scenarios or situations.
4. Immediately, the volunteers will perform these scenarios (as a group) in the manner of the adverb.
5. Aim of your group is to accurately predict the adverb the volunteers are performing as quickly as possible.
6. If the correct adverb has not been guessed within 10 seconds, your group will offer a new scenario.
7. Play continues, with a series of scenarios and acts until the adverb is identified.
8. Play several rounds, or try a variation.

Variations

- The people acting can only mime their performance in the manner of the word or adverb.
- One or more volunteers leave the room. The rest of the group decides which adverb they will perform. The volunteers return to the playing space, and describe a series of 'situations' for the whole group to act out. Works best if the volunteers stand in the middle of the action.

Reflection

- How difficult was it to think of an adverb?
- What was one of the most difficult adverb scenarios to perform? Why?
- How did the volunteers respond when the group was clearly confused?

Come To My Party

*Curious & fun lateral-thinking game
for large groups.*

Benefits

- Develops critical-thinking
- Promotes creativity
- Sharpens listening skills
- Multiple variations

People 8+

Time   10-15 mins

Instructions

1. Gather your group together, close enough so everyone can hear one another.
2. Each person's task is to identify the 'key' which unlocks the secret to a puzzle.
3. Announce that you're hosting an imaginary party, and everyone is invited.
4. To attend, every person must bring some 'thing' with them. It can be a food, a prop or even a person.
5. Next, invite a series of volunteers to nominate what they would like to bring to your party.
6. Here's the key: the 'thing' must be spelled with two consecutive letters that are the same to be acceptable.
7. Unless a person brings the correct thing, eg beer, strawberries, Darren, they can not attend the party.
8. As each person makes an attempt to uncover the key, congratulate those who get it, and encourage those who do not.
9. Continue to offer more and more obvious clues until everyone has identified the key.

Variation

- Vary the key, eg the first letter of the 'thing' will conform to the alphabet, eg Avocado, Beans, Carrot, Durian, etc, or the thing must have one particular type of letter, such as the letter A, somewhere within it's spelling.

Reflection

- Did you put yourself under any pressure to crack the code?
- What was the trigger that finally unlocked the key for you?
- How might we show empathy towards others who are yet to unlock the key?

Bang, You're Dead

*Curious lateral-thinking game
for small & large groups.*

Benefits

- Ideal time-filler
- Develops critical-thinking
- Sharpens listening skills
- Multiple variations

People 12+

Time 10-15 mins

Instructions

1. Assemble your group in front of you, perhaps in a circle.
2. Each person's task is to identify the 'key' which unlocks the secret to a puzzle.
3. To start, point your finger to any individual in the group and say "BANG, YOU'RE DEAD."
4. After some moments have passed, ask your group to nominate who it is you eliminated.
5. Allow for two or more people to predict who was eliminated.
6. Here's the key: the first person to speak after you have said the word "...DEAD" is eliminated.
7. As each person makes an attempt to uncover the key, congratulate those who get it, and encourage those who do not.
8. Continue to offer more and more obvious clues until everyone has identified the key.

Variations

- For those working in a zero-tolerance environment, substitute key words with "SURPRISE" or any other acceptable sounding statement.
- Sit with your legs crossed (or uncrossed) making sure that your right (or left) foot is pointing to a particular individual (ie the dead person.) So for each round, you adjust your sitting (foot) position, say the magic words, and then sift through the various guesses until the deceased is identified correctly.

Reflection

- How fast did you work out what was going on?
- How did it feel to be one of the last to 'get it?'
- When was the last time you felt like this? Was there a positive outcome?

part three

RESOURCES
& SUPPORT

CHAPTER 15

Here To Help You

The remainder of this book is focused on helping you to make the most of the content shared within the previous chapters. It made sense to separate this valuable information from the main body of the text so as to not interrupt the flow of the conversation.

First, I'll share more details about three extremely valuable tools to help you make successful program design and leadership decisions. Then, even more valuable, I share the building-blocks of forty ready-to-play program templates and links to a bunch of free resources (smartphone app, video tutorials, articles, etc.)

Finally, to help answer some of your questions – or perhaps to subscribe, enrol or register for one of several professional development offerings – I share my contact details.

1. Smart Goals

As discussed in Chapter 3, a poor process to setting an effective goal, or worse, the absence of a goal, are two of the main reasons programs fail.

In my goal-setting endeavours, I have found it useful to follow the SMART goal guidelines to set effective goals. SMART goals are:

- **S** Specific – clear and concise, one goal at a time
- **M** Measurable – in time and quantity
- **A** Achievable – realistic, but also a stretch
- **R** Relevant – has direct significance and connection
- **T** Trackable – allows monitoring of progress

Program goals come in many shapes and sizes, and may sound like 'to improve leadership skills' or 'increase confidence' or 'develop team-skills.'

While admirable, these goals are not particularly effective because it is very difficult to know if you have achieved them or not. They do not meet the characteristics of a SMART goal.

To illustrate the difference, here is a SMART goal that has been developed for a three-hour 'get-to-know-you' session for a group of new employees: Everyone will recall at least two things about ten other people by the end of the session.

This goal is SMART because it is (S) focused on one clearly defined goal, (M) measured in terms of people, recall and time, (A) will stretch the capabilities of the team, (R) important because it will fast-track the development of a new project team, and (T) by the end of the session, the team will know if the goal was achieved, or not.

Here's a real-life example of the impact of setting an effective goal.

A group of dysfunctional young people were forced to attend a weekend camp. Following a series of high-energy, fun activities, my colleagues and I helped the young people set two SMART goals. In their own words, their most immediate goal was to 'go back home,' which, in time, we could promise would be achieved. However, we worked with them to set a second goal – to have fun. This had all the hallmarks of a SMART goal – specific, easy to measure, was certainly achievable and was trackable. But the key to its success was the R, relevance – this goal mattered to the young people because the alternative was to endure a miserable couple of days at camp before they could achieve their first goal (go home.) This second goal framed every interaction and conversation we had from that point on. There is no doubt, that without this second goal, we would have been butting heads all weekend.

Remember, having a goal is not the same as making a difference. Turn to Chapter 4 to study the essential task of articulating a difference in more detail.

2. GRABBSS

One of the most commonly asked questions from program providers is 'How do I know if I'm using the right activity at the right time?'

Adopting a sequenced approach to your program requires an ability to assess and read your group at any given time. In the interests of selecting the right activity at the right time, I can think of no better instrument than GRABBSS.

Created by Project Adventure, GRABBSS is a self-assessment tool that you can use to make informed decisions about the 'right' thing to do in any given moment, and when to make adjustments to your program.

GRABBSS is a series of questions divided across seven key elements you can observe and evaluate about your group. One element is not necessarily more important than another, but the acronym reads as follows:

Goals What is the purpose of this activity? How does this experience relate to the goals of the group? Will it make a difference to the group?

Readiness Is the group ready (mentally, emotionally, physically) to undertake the experience? What needs to change before the group has the ability to undertake the next stage of the program?

Affect What is the feeling of the group? What sensations are they experiencing – boredom, excitement, apathy, resistance, etc? How do these feelings impact what they do next?

Behaviour How are the group or individuals acting? Are the interactions among members positive or negative for the group? How co-operative are they? Will their behaviour be appropriate for their next experience?

Body What are the physical abilities of the group? What physical characteristics of the group will impact the program? Are the individuals tired, do they look after their bodies, do any individuals have a disability, are they hot or cold, etc?

Stage What stage of development is the group experiencing? It is useful to refer to Bruce Tuckman's popular rhyming schema to describe the varying levels:

- Forming – beginning of a group's existence, most activity fits within Comfort Zone;
- Storming – often involves conflict as individuals start to assert their opinions and leadership;
- Norming – group cohesion is forming, as it identifies more productive ways to function;
- Performing – group is functioning effectively and efficiently; and
- Transforming – the point at which the group ceases to exist.

Does your group need additional skills to function at a higher level (stage) of development? Generally speaking, the higher the level of group development, the more challenging your experience can be.

Setting What is the physical setting of the program and the 'cultural' background of the participants? Are you inside or outside, secluded or likely to be disturbed? Is the space limited? How long have the people known or worked with each other?

In essence, you are constantly asking yourself these types of questions to help you make an informed decision about what is appropriate or 'right' for your group as you proceed.

For example, you may be working with a school group for the purposes of developing problem-solving skills. Even though the agenda indicates that you should do a particular activity straight after the break, if the group has not demonstrated that it has the skills necessary to succeed, ie the group is not ready, then you are well advised to alter your program sequence. Slot in some extra activities to better prepare your group, or present an alternative exercise in place of the less-appropriate one.

Or, perhaps the group is ready to move onto the next experience, but has 'cooled' down significantly during your debrief. Then, throw in a quick 'warm-up' to move their bodies once again before proceeding.

3. Spotting Skills

In Chapter 12, I introduce a term referred to as 'spotting.' Spotting is the activity of securing and protecting the physical well-being of a person engaged in an adventurous activity.

In practice, it may look like breaking or catching a person's fall, but it may also be as simple as being alert for potentially harmful events or things.

As a program develops, the momentum to assume bigger challenges – that is, greater perceived and actual risks – often increases. This may encourage an individual or group to step outside their Comfort Zones and assume more physically demanding and harmful activities.

Naturally, as program leaders, we are called to facilitate a safe outcome on these occasions, but there is enormous value in empowering our groups to help us shoulder this responsibility. And this is where spotting skills comes in.

Spotting is perhaps one of the most difficult tasks to teach because, in most cases, people do not recognise the importance of being a spotter until it's too late, ie someone falls or is hurt. It's a bit like shutting the gate after the horse has bolted. Well, indulge me for a few moments as I briefly introduce the fence to you.

Here are some key aspects to remember when teaching effective spotting skills:

- A safe spotting stance will require the spotter to be balanced with one foot in front of the other, knees flexed to absorb impact, eyes forward, elbows bent and their hands up in a ready position, ie the Bumpers Up position.
- A series of common calls or commands are recommended to prepare everybody before action, such as:

  Participant: "Are you ready?"

  Spotter: "Yes, I am ready."

  Participant: "I'm ready to walk (run, fall, whatever.)"

  Spotter: "Walk (run, fall, whatever) away."

- Spotters will follow and mimic the movements of the participant and remain with them until the activity concludes.
- Spotting should focus on 'breaking' or supporting a fall, not necessarily catching the participant.
- The head, neck and upper torso are the highest priority for a spotter.
- Spotting is not helping or assisting the participant complete their task.

The activities listed under the heading Spotting Skills Sequence (Chapter 12) will introduce a number of fun and fully-functional activities to help you teach good spotting skills.

CHAPTER 16

Ready-To-Play Program Templates

Often the hardest part of designing and leading a program is knowing where to start.

While there are clear risks in becoming too prescriptive, there is value in sharing a series of program templates which have worked for me, and – perhaps with a little tweaking on your end – will work for you, too.

Here are forty simple programs to get you started.

Instructions for all of the activities referenced below can be found in this book. As an added benefit, you can view short video tutorials for all of them, and so much more, at **playmeo.com/activities**

In an effort to provide something for everyone, most of these templates are for programs of 10, 30 and 60 minutes and invite groups of 12, 30 and 100 people to play. Naturally, no equipment is necessary!

Large Group Energisers

Simple, fun exercises ideally suited to large groups of people, often situated in restricted and/or seated environments.

	1 min	2 mins	5 mins	10 mins
100 people	Gotcha	Your Add	PDQ Test	Story Of Your Name Wiggle Waggle

Get-To-Know-You Programs

Highly-interactive sessions which invite a group of strangers to get to know one another. Emphasis on non-threatening fun, mixing and sharing.

	10 mins	30 mins	60 mins
12 people	Five Handshakes in Five Minutes Gotcha	Spectrums Me You You Me Identity Crisis	Thumb Wrestling In Stereo Me You You Me Imaginary Toss-A-Name Game What's In A Name?
30 people	Ice-Breaker Question Exchange	Who? Categories Psychic Handshake	Crosstown Connections One-Two-Three Story Of Your Name Name Roulette
100 people	Let Me Introduce Tiny Teach	Vortex ESP Cocktail Party	Train Station Greetings Kram Dralloc Clumps Must Choose

Fun, Community-Building Programs

Fun, highly-interactive group-based sessions which strengthen relationships and generate lots of energy. Ideal for weekly and evening programs for new and established groups.

	10 mins	30 mins	60 mins
12 people	Ro Sham Bo Paired Shares	Fill Me In Wah Ah So Ko	One Duck Zip Zap Follow The Leader In the Manner Of The Word
30 people	One-Two-Three	Speed Rabbit Have You Ever?	Fill The Space Mission Impossible Finding Nemo The Story Game
100 people	1-2-3-4 Space Counting	Evolution People To People Coming & Going Of The Rain	Categories Mirror Stretch Slap Bang This Or That Chic-A-Boom

Team-Development Programs

Interactive sessions which purposefully build and strengthen relationships. Emphasis on the development of trust, communication and problem-solving skills.

	10 mins	30 mins	60 mins
12 people	Mute Line-Up	Look Up Look Down Quick Shuffle	Elevator Air Making Connections Yurt Circle Span The Room
30 people	Funny Walk	Isometric Stretch Everybody Up Body English	Spot The Difference Palm Off Trust Leans Trust Line
100 people	Vortex	Snoopy & Red Baron Star Stretch	Spectrums Ice-Breaker Question Exchange ESP Hog Call Lap Circle

Warm-Up & High-Energy Programs

Full-on, high-energy sessions which aim to raise a sweat and a lot of smiles.

	5 mins	10 mins	20 mins
12 people	I've Got The Power	Everybody Is It Hospital Tag	Skipping Rope Quick Line-Up
30 people	Finger Fencing Toe Tag	Giants Wizards Elves	Fill The Space Freeze Frame
100 people	Triangle Tag	Walk Tag	Knee Tag Shipwreck

Looking For More?

These forty sample programs are just the beginning.

Browse playmeo's activity database to create your own bespoke programs and explore hundreds more outrageously fun group games and activities to enjoy.

Go to **playmeo.com/activities**

CHAPTER 17

Useful Resources

First of all, thank you for taking the time to read this book.

I hope you have enjoyed everything that I have shared between its covers. My sole intention was to share a bunch of really useful activity ideas and skills that can help you deliver remarkably fun group games and activities - with no equipment whatsoever.

Now, I'm sure you've got questions or need further guidance. This book, nor any book, could possibly answer every question you have about making a difference to the groups you work with.

Maybe you have a question about one or more the activities I shared?

Maybe you need help to find the perfect activity for your next program?

Or, maybe you're seeking some form of professional development to further enhance your program leadership skills?

In 2012, I founded the company playmeo with a vision to inspire, equip and empower leaders (like you) with the skills and strategies they need to become better group leaders and facilitators.

In this spirit, and when you are ready, I encourage you to browse, download, subscribe and enrol in one or more of the following practical resources.

Free Group Games App

Download the playmeo Group Games & Activities app (search for 'playmeo') onto your smart device from your favourite app marketplace (iOS and Android.) It curates all of playmeo's free content, including dozens of group games & activities, video tutorials, leadership advice and weekly blog posts.

Online Group Games & Activities Database

Browse the largest online activity database in the world – **playmeo.com** – to find the perfect activity for your group's needs. Hundreds of ice-breakers, energisers, trust exercises and team-building & problem-solving activities, featuring step-by-step instructions, video tutorials, variations, leadership and reflection tips. Browse for free, or subscribe to access all of the premium content.

Facilitator Tips Video Tutorials

playmeo posts a short, two-minute video every fortnight which focuses on the art and science of group facilitation skills. Ideal for beginners who don't know where to start, and experienced practitioners who are looking to be inspired with new ideas. Each episode is accompanied by useful links, bonus resources and a video transcript. And best of all – they're free. Visit **playmeo.com/facilitatortips**

Training Workshops

Attend one of our open-enrolment workshops, or we'll come to you and deliver a custom-designed program just for you and your group. Lead by one of playmeo's international team of expert facilitators, our clients tell us these practical training workshops are the most powerful and rewarding professional development courses they ever do. Options range from one-day introductory programs to advanced multi-day workshops which can be custom-designed for your particular training needs. Visit **playmeo.com/professional-development**

One-on-One Coaching

A series of regular live coaching calls with one of playmeo's international team of experts are designed to reinforce the content of a practical training workshop you experienced or to help you manage a range of opportunities or issues in your new or existing programs. You can book a single session or lock into one of our popular 3, 6 or 12-month plans. Visit **playmeo.com/professional-development**

Online Tutorials

If turning up is difficult to arrange, then consider registering for one of our self-paced online tutorials. These short, innovative online programs are designed for leaders who don't know where to start, or have just begun leading groups and need some practical advice. Your learning modules can be accessed 24/7 on any internet-enabled device and may be repeated as often as you wish. Ideal for beginners, but equally valuable for experienced practitioners who are looking to 'sharpen the saw.' Visit **playmeo.com/online-learning-course**

Acknowledgements

As I have shared in my earlier books, gratitude is one of the most powerful emotions one can bring into their life and offer to others.

For this, my fifth major publication, I offer my deepest gratitude to the following people:

Gilly and **Devon**, my family. I couldn't ask for a more loving, caring environment in which to support my writing and playing. As always, I love you, and thank you.

Karl Rohnke, once again. You continue to inspire me, with not only the near and far influence you have had on my program leadership skills, but also with the legacy of your playful words bound in the many books you have written over the years. Thank you, my friend.

Anna Rampelt, for creating a family of little people and characters which bring the book alive. You deciphered hundreds of my hand-sketched stick-figures and diagrams to bless this book (and playmeo's online resources) with an abundance of illustrations which capture the essence of every activity.

Every practitioner with whom I have worked over the past 30+ years, including **Bill**, **Steve**, **Tania**, **Leslie**, **Jane**, **Mary**, **Mark**, **Paul**, **David**, **Nate**, **Ryan**, **Adam**, **Lisa**, **Rich**, **Tara**, **Allison**, **Jim**, **Michelle**, **Chris** and **Sam**. Always a treat to watch, observe and learn from you all.

John and **Faye Grave**, for taking a three-week vacation at just the right time so that I could borrow your distraction-free, upstairs study to pen most of this book.

Michelle Pirovich, for once again wrestling with many thousands of words and hundreds of images and helping them all play so nicely together.

And finally, to the many, many people I have had the privilege to work and play with over the years. What a pleasure and honour it has been to share with you.

Thank you.

About The Author

Mark Collard is one of the most experienced and respected experiential educators and training consultants in the world. He is an expert at helping program leaders design and deliver remarkably fun programs that make a difference in the lives and performance of their groups.

Mark is the author of three top-selling activity publications:

No Props: Great Games with No Equipment (2005)

Count Me In: Large Group Activities That Work (2008)

Serious Fun: Your Step-by-Step Guide to Leading Remarkably Fun Programs That Make a Difference (2014)

In 2012, he launched playmeo.com, an innovative online platform that equips program leaders around the world with access to a variety of online resources, practical training workshops and one-on-one coaching programs. playmeo is best known for hosting the largest online group activity database in the world.

Mark brings a natural warmth and energy to everything he delivers. His fun and vibrant approach not only makes people feel at home, but also assists them to learn more from their experience.

A highly sought-after trainer on the national and international circuit, Mark is also a fun and super-passionate keynote speaker, voice-over professional and Master of Ceremonies.

On a personal note, Mark has been struck by lightning twice, he has found five four-leafed clovers (so far) and estimates that he has spent more than six months of his life (so far) sitting inside a steel tube hurtling through the air at 800 kph as he has criss-crossed the globe on his travels.

Mark lives with his beautiful wife and son in Melbourne's outer east, and counts his time travelling and delivering programs with groups all over the world as some of the most rewarding and funnest times of his life.

Contact Mark

Mark would love to hear from you.

Please reach out to him if you have any questions, or would like to learn more about his books, online resources, training workshops and one-on-one coaching programs.

 PO Box 4237, Croydon Hills VIC 3136, Australia

 +61 413 075 123

 www.playmeo.com

 hello@playmeo.com

 @playmeo

 www.facebook.com/playmeo

 playmeo

 www.playmeo.com/mark-collard

 www.markcollard.com

References

I stand on the shoulders of many giants when it comes to acknowledging the many influences I have benefited from during my career.

Here is just a short list of resources, experts and references which have inspired many an expansive thought and scaffolded the conclusions I share in this publication:

Books

Silver Bullets: A Guide To Initiative Problems, Adventure Games & Trust Activities, by Karl Rohnke (2010)

Quicksilver: Adventure Games, Initiative Problems, Trust Activities & A Guide To effective Leadership, by Karl Rohnke & Steve Butler (1995)

FUNN 'n Games: Adventure Games, Initiatives & Trust Activities for FUNN & Facilitation, by Karl Rohnke (2004)

No Props: Great Games with No Equipment, by Mark Collard (2005)

Count Me In: Large Group Activities That Work, by Mark Collard (2008)

Serious Fun: Your Step-by-Step Guide to Leading Remarkably Fun Programs That Make a Difference, by Mark Collard (2014)

The Hundredth Monkey: Activities That Inspire Playful Learning, by Nate Folan & friends (2012)

Organisations & Experts

Partnership for 21st Century Learning, non-profit organisation that aims to build collaborative partnerships among education, business, community and government leaders.
p21.org

Dr Stuart Brown, founder, National Institute for Play and author of play.
nifp.org

Zones of Proximal Development, first developed by psychologist Lev Vygotsky (1986-1934).
wikipedia.org/wiki/zone_of_proximal_development

Development sequence in small groups, by Bruce Tuckman (1965).
en.wikipedia.org/wiki/Tuckman%27s_stages_of_group_development

David Kolb, originator of the Experiential Learning Model.
wikipedia.org/wiki/experiential_learning

Dr William Glasser, American psychiatrist, (1925-2013)
en.wikipedia.org/wiki/William_Glasser

George Burr Leonard, American writer, editor & educator (1923-2010).
en.wikipedia.org/wiki/George_Leonard

Research, Articles & Studies

Australian Temperament Project: The first 30 years, Australian institute of Family Studies, edited by Suzanne Vassallo & Ann Sanson (2013).
aifs.gov.au/publications/australian-temperament-project

A 32-Year Longitudinal Study of Child and Adolescent Pathways to Well-Being in Adulthood, Journal of Happiness Studies, by Craig Olsson, Rob McGee, Shyamala Nada-Raja & Sheila M. Williams (2012).
dunedinstudy.otago.ac.nz/publications

A meta-analysis of outdoor adventure programming with adolescents. Journal of Experiential Education, by Dana Cason & Lee Gillis (1994).
dx.doi.org/10.1177/105382599401700109

Adventure education and Outward Bound: Out-of-class experiences that make a lasting difference. Review of Educational Research, by John Hattie, H Marsh, James Neill & Garry Richards (1997).
dx.doi.org/10.3102/00346543067001043

A meta-analysis of outdoor education programs, by James Laidlaw (2000). Available from ProQuest Dissertations & Theses Global.

How are adventure education program outcomes achieved? A review of the literature, Australian Journal of Outdoor Education, by M McKenzie (2000). Available from ProQuest Dissertations & Theses Global.

Using Social, Emotional & Character Development to Improve Academic Outcomes: A Matched Pair, Cluster Randomized Controlled Trial in Low Income, Urban Schools. Journal of School Health, by Niloofar Bavarian, Kendra Lewis, David Dubois, Alan Acock, Samual Vuchinich, Naida Silverthorn, Frank Snyder, Joseph Day, Peter Ji & Brian Flay (2013).
dx.doi.org/10.1111/josh.12093

The positive impact of social and emotional learning for kindergarten to eighth grade students, Chicago, IL: Collaborative for Academic, Social, and Emotional Learning (CASEL) by John Payton, Roger Weissberg, Joseph Durlak, Allison Dymnicki, Rebecca Taylor, Kriston Schellinger & Molly Pachan (2008).
files.eric.ed.gov/fulltext/ED505370.pdf

Effectiveness of school-based universal social, emotional, and behavioral programs: Do they enhance students' development in the area of skill, behavior & adjustment? Psychology in the Schools, Marcin Sklad, Rene Diekstra, Monique Ritter, Jehonathan Ben & Carolien Gravesteijn (2012).
dx.doi.org/10.1002/pits.21641

Index – Interpersonal Skills

The four critical interpersonal skills, known as the 4 x Cs, are communication, collaboration, critical-thinking and creativity. To assist you in your planning processes, every activity described in this book is listed under one of these four key skills.

Naturally, all four skills are interdependent, but the purpose of these lists is to identify which one of the four key skills could be the primary focus or benefit of each activity. Of course this estimation is purely subjective, so feel free to disregard at will.

Communication

Collaboration

Critical-Thinking

Creativity

Index – Alphabetical

Notes & Doodles

Notes & Doodles

Notes & Doodles

CPSIA information can be obtained
at www.ICGtesting.com
Printed in the USA
JSHW061232050623
42697JS00001B/4

9 780992 546427